THE SCRIPTURE UNION GUIDE TO RUNNING HOLIDAY CLUBS, TERM-TIME MISSIONS AND OTHER SPECIAL EVENTS

Steve Hutchinson

Scripture Union

Thanks to...

Eric Hayden for his continued encouragement to me to complete this book.
Janet Morgan, Paul Butler and Vic Lanchester for their helpful comments.
Alison Barr for accepting the idea, and Josephine Campbell for her editing skills
and patience with me.

Scripture Union, 207–209 Queensway, Bletchley, Milton Keynes, MK2 2EB, England.

© Steve Hutchinson 1996

First published 1996

ISBN 1 85999 016 9

British Library Cataloguing-in-Publication Data
A catalogue record for this book is available from the British Library.

Cover design by Tony Cantale Graphics.
Design and illustration by Tony Cantale Graphics.

Printed and bound in Great Britain by Ebenezer Baylis & Son Limited,
The Trinity Press, Worcester and London.

CONTENTS

Before you begin...   4

1 Children   5
Understanding children. The importance of building friendships.
Sharing the Good News with children.

2 What's it all about?   7
What happens at a special outreach event – small groups, 'all together' times.

3 Initial decisions   9
Prayer. Aims – why do you want a holiday club? Assessing previous missions.
Finance. Children's age range. Pros & cons of holding an event in the holidays
or term-time. Weekend events. Venue. Theme. People. Inviting an evangelist.
Training. Working with other churches.

4 Planning details   18
Planning meetings. Choosing your team. The programme –
children's response, music. Publicity. Dedication service. Equipment.
The Children Act 1989 – sample letter to local authority. Special needs.
First Aid. Insurance. Safety. Storing information. Follow-up.

5 During the event   28
Prayer. Discipline. Family events. Family service.

6 After the event   32
More people coming? Assessing the event.

7 TaskSheets   34
A. Check-lists.
B. Prayer.
C. Publicity.
D. School liaison.
E. Programme.
F. People.
G. Follow-up.
H. Catering.

Appendix 1: A visiting evangelist   62

Appendix 2: Addresses for resources and book list   63

BEFORE YOU BEGIN...

NUTS & BOLTS is designed to help churches who want to run special outreach events for children and their families. Nuts & Bolts is not theme-based in the way that other Scripture Union holiday club publications are. Rather, the book fits alongside these to provide help in planning the activities and organisation of outreach events, and to give lots of ideas, hints and details on running them.

Nuts & Bolts has grown out of the notes produced for missions I have been involved in over the last fourteen years. People co-ordinating the missions found that these notes provided information and ideas unavailable elsewhere. Some of this information relates closely to the way in which I like to work, but much of it will be of use generally.

'A special outreach event' is the all-embracing term I use to include holiday clubs, term-time missions and 'family fun' events at weekends. The essential nature of any of these is that we invite children and their families to join in activities which help us all to understand the Bible better and respond to its message. Most of these events will be evangelistic in that the people invited are those who don't already come to church.

A special outreach event needs someone, a co-ordinator, to make sure things happen, to keep an overall record of decisions taken and who is doing what where, and so on. **Nuts & Bolts** is an especially useful resource for that co-ordinator.

Nuts & Bolts contains a number of sections, and so reflects the stages of preparation required for an outreach event. You don't need to read it all! Choose a section as it fits your needs. The first after this introduction is concerned with the initial decision to hold a holiday club or mission. If you have already made that decision, skip this and move on to the next section, which deals with planning the event in detail. TaskSheets (see pp 34–61) outline the jobs to be delegated at each stage – these may be photocopied and distributed. In a smaller church or club event you may not need to use all the TaskSheets, but they can help you with ideas.

Nuts & Bolts is designed to be a worker's tool. Take this book with you to meetings. Scribble in the margins. Fill in the check-lists. Photocopy and use the prayer bookmarks, publicity material, and so on. Please don't feel constrained by the ideas and ways of working proposed in **Nuts & Bolts**. These are just suggestions to get you started, and you may adapt the material as you wish. Instead, let this book stimulate your thinking about the way you organise special outreach events.

Steve Hutchinson

CHILDREN

Children often seem naturally nearer to God than adults. Get talking to children about God and you get some very interesting questions: 'Who made God?' 'Is God a man?' 'Is Jesus God or is God God?' 'Why did God make Jesus die?' We can help children to find the answers to these questions as we share with them from the Bible. However, quick and easy answers often won't satisfy their curiosity; it is only through relationships and conversations developed over time that the full truth of the gospel will become clear to them.

Jesus said, 'Let the children come to me and do not stop them, because the Kingdom of heaven belongs to such as these' (Matthew 19:14, Good News Bible) A little earlier in Matthew's Gospel, in chapter 18, we have what some call 'The Children's Charter': everyone who works with children should read this. I am particularly challenged by verse 5: 'Whoever welcomes in my name one such child as this, welcomes me'.

What are children like?

Children are lively and active, often demanding of our attention. They have a short attention span and can't concentrate for too long on anything. They will soon let you know if they are bored! In fact, boredom is sometimes the cause of bad behaviour. One colleague of mine likes to 'keep the programme moving so fast their feet don't touch the ground!'

Friends are very important to children – they want to be with their friends and do the same things. We must remember this when we share the Good News with children and when we are putting them into small groups during holiday club activities. If friends or siblings on different sides of the age divide want to stay together, they should be allowed to.

Children are part of a family, and we must be careful to remember this too. We should earn the trust of parents and not do anything to harm the relationship between them and their children.

Of course, children's experience is generally more limited than adults'. I can remember when England won the World Cup! And when man first stepped on the moon. For children these events are nearly ancient history. Their experience of travel is also limited – some will have been abroad, others will not.

Children generally learn faster than grown-ups, but pre-teens may not understand many of the abstract concepts of the Christian faith that grown-ups take for granted, like 'faith'. They need things explained in concrete terms. When we share the Good News with them, we must demonstrate what we mean using examples or things that they already comprehend.

Books by Scripture Union that will help further with understanding children:

Under-Fives Welcome! (about under-5s, amazingly!) by Kathleen Crawford

Become Like a Child (working with 5-7+) by Kathryn Copsey

Help! There's a Child in my Church (working with 8-10+) by Peter Graystone

Outside In (working with teens) by Mike Breen

Friendship evangelism

The starting point for any outreach to children will be making friends with them. We want them to feel welcome and at home in our church. This will affect how we organise the venue and what sort of programme we run.

Building relationships with children is even more important if you are inviting an outside evangelist. Children may get very attached to the evangelist and be sorry when he or she leaves. However, if the children have got to know some church members, the situation will be much better. Of course, this means that more must be asked of the home-team members than just to be there for the event. Ideally they should be regular attendees of the church, not necessarily involved in the children's work but there often enough to see the children after the event is over.

It will take time on our part to get to know the children who come to our churches. Many adults have little time for children nowadays; yet one of the most important experiences for a child is that of forming positive, dependable relationships. As children come to know us, and as we share our lives with them, we hope that they will discover what it means to be valued and respected for who they are as individuals. This could be a new experience for some children.

We also hope that children will see the Good News in action as they see something of Jesus in us and realise that Jesus also values them as special people. If you think back to those who helped you become a Christian, I suspect you can remember much more about what they were like than what they said. So it will be with us and the children we meet: how we live is more important than what we say.

The message

We share the Good News that Jesus came to bring. It is so simple that a child can respond to it, and yet so deep none of us fully understands it. Paul used a variety of ways to explain the Good News to people: for example, the Courtroom (Romans 3:19–31; Galatians 3:1–29), from which we get the idea of being 'justified' or acquitted because Jesus has taken the punishment we deserve; and the Slave Market (Romans 6:15–23) from which we get the idea of being 'redeemed' from our slavery to sin because Jesus has paid the price for our freedom by dying on the cross.

Likewise, we can use different ways to explain the gospel. For example, I often speak of Jesus the Friend and invite the children to ask to be friends with Jesus. Alternatively, the theme for the mission could be 'Jesus the Leader', looking at how people followed him. This would lead to an invitation for us to follow him too. In using these approaches we must be careful not to omit the fundamentals of the Good News. We are not encouraging children to carry on as they are and join another club. Rather, the Good News requires a change in all our lives as we respond to it.

Children may not fully understand repentance, but they can be encouraged to say sorry to God and mean it. They may not understand everything about us needing Jesus to be our Lord and Saviour, or about the Holy Spirit's power filling us, but we must work at explaining these things so that children can respond. There are people today who complain that they were 'badly born' as Christians because those who led them to Christ missed out parts of the Good News.

Books by Scripture Union that give a fuller explanation of how children can grow in faith:

Reaching Children and **Reaching Families** by Paul Butler   **Children Finding Faith** by Francis Bridger (this book is now out of print but is very useful if you can get a copy)

2
WHAT'S IT ALL ABOUT?

I remember visiting one church to discuss a special outreach week where they kept talking about a holiday club they had run the previous summer. Now I assumed they meant a week of club activities, with songs, Bible stories, crafts, and so on. Actually, they had run a single day of fun and games but called it a 'holiday club'! So here's an expansion of what I mean by a special outreach event and some of the things that could go on during one.

First, a holiday club takes place during the school holidays, and a term-time mission or Bible club during the school term. Amazing, isn't it?! Both types of events are good tools for outreach to children and their families. Chapter three, 'Initial Decisions', discusses the pros and cons of these two types of events, but what happens at them? What do you do?

All the special events that I lead include times when the children are separated into small groups and times when they meet together *en masse*.

Small groups

The time that the children spend in groups together during a special event programme is vital. Working within a 'small group' structure is a helpful 'way in' for adults to make friendships with them. Activities done together, such as drawing, writing, colouring or making things, help to build relationships. The children will get to know their group leader who can then encourage them to carry on coming after the event is over. Group times also serve to reinforce the message that we are sharing with the children. In their groups they have an opportunity to ask questions and chat about the Bible stories or drama they have seen, and it is certainly easier for a child to read the Bible or pray aloud in a small group than to a large crowd of everyone all together. And funsheets can be given out: 'Funsheets are what we do in the club where we have fun; worksheets are what we do in school where we work!'

On mine I usually include simple puzzles, quizzes on Bible verses, pictures to colour, a 'think spot' and a prayer; the aim is to help the children think a little more about the story or theme for that day. If you are following a programme from published holiday club material, 'small group' times are particularly good for doing crafts that highlight the programme's theme, eg mobiles, making a newspaper, collage, kites, puppets, and all sorts of other things.

'All together' times

The children meet together *en masse* to sing songs, watch the drama, join in quizzes and listen to Bible stories. They feel part of something bigger, and this makes it all more exciting. The content of the 'all together' time has to be suitable for all the children, however, so it should be fast-moving and varied. In general, one item should last no more than a few minutes, say ten minutes at the most. The next item will follow on immediately, with no breaks. Sometimes activities in a programme can be separated by songs, eg song – prayer – song – quiz – song – memory verse – song – Bible story.

The Bible story or drama you choose will usually be based on the theme you are following. This may come from a publication such as **Chattabox** or **Newshounds**, two of Scripture Union's holiday club programmes, or it may be a theme you have worked out yourself. In each case, check carefully that the stories are suitable for the age and background of the children you are expecting to come. Those with little church background will need a more careful explanation when a Bible story is told. Make sure that the ideas involved are within the children's ability to understand. One young evangelist got very excited about the stories in Judges and all the heroes there, until it was pointed out that Jephthah promised to sacrifice a person (it ended up being his daughter) and Samson slept around all over the place. Neither of these stories are ideal for children, let alone sensitive young children or those with no Bible knowledge.

Quizzes are good if used well. They allow the team and the children to have fun together. Team members can ask questions to discover what the children know already or to see what they remember from the previous day. I usually play a game on a large board to add to the fun. Be careful not to wind the children up too much as they can become very competitive. However, quizzes are generally very popular. Try to include some easy questions, some that don't come from the Bible, and to ask different children each time, not just the ones who always put their hands up. I remember offering to do quizzes for an evangelist I was working with, who replied that he didn't use quizzes much with younger children because they were a bit trivial. I went ahead and used my games for fun, asking questions to reinforce the previous day's message. At the end of the mission he seemed quite pleased if not totally converted to the idea!

I love to teach memory verses, though I usually call them 'Brain-stretchers' now. I choose a simple verse that fits the theme and teach that, using words on cards, a jigsaw, a rap or a song. Even young children can learn them well if they are taught properly. Bible verses learned young will stick with children forever. There is more on all these 'all together' items in the book **Help! I Want to Tell Kids About Jesus** (Scripture Union).

If you run a shorter outreach event, you may not be able to include everything, but you should be able to have at least one 'all together' session and one session in groups. Typical programmes can be found on TaskSheet E.

INITIAL DECISIONS

The first time you meet to discuss a holiday club, mission or special outreach event, everyone who is interested should be allowed to have their say. Some people will come with reservations; others will not be sure what is meant by, say, a holiday club.

To allow for a reasonable amount of time for planning and preparation, the decision to hold the event should really be made approximately nine to ten months before the proposed date. Holding a special outreach event is a big undertaking that can cost a lot of time and money, so it is important to think it through before you become too committed.

Prayer

In anything we do, we want to be sure we are doing God's will, especially if we are organising a special event in his name. It is easy to agree with this in theory, but more difficult to work it out in practice. So often prayer is left until last in our discussions. You might consider calling the whole church to a period of prayer to discover God's mind, before deciding to go ahead. Then, when the decision to go ahead has been made, there should be ongoing prayer for the outreach team, the **venue**, the materials, the programme, the publicity and all the other many details involved in holding the event.

Not everyone in the church can take an active part in the planning and organisation, yet their support in prayer is vital. And don't forget the children in your Sunday school. This special outreach event is for children and their families, so they should be included as much as possible. See TaskSheet B for suggestions on encouraging people to pray.

Time to think

Think *why* you want to have the event. Many people are not really sure or have the idea that an event worked well somewhere else so 'we have to do something too'. I remember a preliminary visit I made to one church that asked me to lead a holiday club. It was a dark night and we met in a dingy back room. One of the first questions I asked was, 'Why do you want to have a holiday club?' There was absolute silence for what seemed like ages, then an old man said, 'Eeh, I think you've got us stumped on that one, lad.'

It may be helpful to work out your aims before you start any actual planning and then gauge the success of what you have done by referring to these when the event is over. Here are some possible aims:

- To have a time of concentrated teaching with the children in your Sunday school
- To build up a feeling of belonging together in your Sunday school
- To bring more children into your Sunday school
- To tell children outside the church about Jesus and encourage them to know him for themselves
- To show children that church can be interesting and exciting (not boring!)
- To keep children off the streets
- To reach out to whole families

It is quite possible to satisfy more than one aim, of course, but it is helpful to put them in some kind of order of importance. Keep your aims in mind throughout your planning, and re-state them each time you meet.

Previous missions

If you have held a mission before, it is useful to look back and assess its value before making the decision to have another. What were the aims of your last mission? Did you achieve them? If not, why might this have been? Do you think you had the right aims? One church I visited did good holiday clubs for years with their own children and their friends, but never really reached out to non-church children. When they looked at their aims again, I suggested changing to a term-time mission with school visits. Through doing this they made immediate non-church contacts. I have also visited churches that ran good holiday clubs which produced little long-term fruit. Sometimes we have identified this as being due to ineffective follow-up after the club or lack of real relationship-building with parents.

How do you judge if your previous mission was effective or not? By the number of children who came, or by the number who continue to come to church? By the number who decided to follow Jesus? I don't personally like using numbers as a criterion of success. However, we do need to think carefully so that we don't repeat any mistakes and so that we move on as God leads us.

What about the children who came last time? Are they still following Jesus? Do they still come to church or to the children's activities run by the church? If not, why not? Was the mission at fault, or are there matters to be faced by the church or Sunday school? You want the event you are planning to be the best that it can be. I have led holiday clubs in a few churches where there have been problems. 'Oh yes,' they said, 'It was just like this last year.' Why didn't they tell me? I never asked! So now I do.

Finance

The Bible advises us to count the cost (Luke 14:28–30), so it is wise to spend some time thinking about the expenses involved in running a special event. One church that invited me to lead a holiday club never mentioned money. I don't know if the vicar thought I was coming free and would pay for printing the funsheets, travel, and so on, myself. I was too young and green to raise the matter, so I just handed him a bill as I left on the final Sunday. I received a cheque but never heard from him again!

Contrast this with a small independent church with seemingly limited resources. At every meeting I went to, the treasurer slipped a few notes into my hand to keep me going. He offered me quite a large sum halfway through the term-time club 'for petrol'. When I submitted an account at the end of the week, they paid it immediately, gave a large gift to Scripture Union and insisted that I take all the 'open plate offering' for my ministry. You can imagine I was overwhelmed!

■ Costs

Things to think of budgeting for:

- Resource books (you will need more than one copy of a holiday club publication to operate properly)
- Publicity
- Funsheets, photocopied or printed
- Craft equipment and material such as glue, paint, etc
- Hall hire, heating charge
- Equipment hire (this might include parachute, video projector, videos)
- Refreshments and food
- Prizes

If you are inviting a visiting evangelist, discuss costs with him or her. We wouldn't ask a builder to do major work on a church without an estimate, so why do without one for a mission or holiday club? Please don't ignore the subject of money or wait for the visitor to raise it. Many evangelists can provide a standard letter explaining how they are financed or would be willing to prepare an estimate so that you know the cost in advance.

The most difficult thing to work out is how much to give towards the visitor's upkeep. Some evangelists live by faith, others receive a salary with the organisation supporting them living by faith. You could try guessing the full cost by adding an average weekly salary plus a week's preparation and meetings plus travelling expenses plus secretarial support, Head Office back-up, postage, and so on. (Try doing this before you ask for a figure and you may have less of a shock!) The Scripture Union Missions Department can provide a cost-per-day figure for an evangelist.

Most evangelists never refuse to come on financial grounds and are glad to accept whatever is offered, trusting God to supply their needs.

■ Charging

You must decide whether you want to charge the children for coming. Some churches will be quite happy to do so, but others may feel that this is part of their ministry to the community and will prefer not to. Parents will certainly expect it, so you could surprise them!

If you don't want to charge but parents want to pay, you might consider having an offering to which they can contribute anytime, using specially marked envelopes. It is certainly not unreasonable to ask for a contribution when you have provided a whole morning's activities with crafts, things to take away and refreshments. My personal preference is not to charge but to have a special offering towards expenses that church members and parents may give to if they wish.

What age range?

It is usually best to follow the local school system and run different activities for each age group, eg Infants 4–7s, Juniors 7–11s, Secondary 11–16/18s. Some areas operate the middle school system, so it is as well to know about this.

You can put infants and juniors together, and run an event for 4–11s, but this will mean that some of the younger children will not fully understand what is aimed at the older ones. This problem can be alleviated by making sure that you have a good group time, with the infant-group leaders helping the younger ones through the story, perhaps using funsheets. There is no doubt that the atmosphere of the overall club 'rubs off' on the youngest children, even if they don't fully understand all that is going on.

Some special outreach events opt for separate clubs for 4–7s and 8–11s within the same week. This can work well if there are enough people to help with each age group, as it is unlikely that the mission team will have the time and energy to be involved with both age groups simultaneously.

If there are teenagers (and youth group leaders) who are keen, it would be good to involve them in planning and running special outreach events for younger children. Often teenagers are able to build good informal friendships with children, and the event could provide a valuable training ground for future involvement in children's ministry.

If you want your outreach to be aimed at teenagers, it is usually better to plan something separate especially for them. Experience suggests that the most effective way to get this age group to come to an event is by having a friend invite them. Whatever form your outreach event takes, it should fit in with a regular pattern of youth meetings. Suggested activities include opening a coffee bar with computer, snooker or electronic

games; a 'silly games' evening; barbecues; outings, eg ice skating, swimming, or any other unusual activity that might appeal to them. I have a variety of stand-bys. One is pyrography – burning patterns into wood with a special machine – to make door plaques and name plates. (Some schools have a machine for this; I built my own and lend it out.) Another is a food evening, with mixed up sandwiches to guess blindfolded (eg peanut butter, lettuce and Marmite, or rice pudding, cheese and lemon curd!), and the girls (blindfolded) feeding the boys ice cream and jelly afterwards. I follow this with the story of Daniel and his friends not eating the king's food, using the video **Daniel & Co** (Scripture Union).

Holiday or term-time?

Most special outreach events run for a week, with a daily programme of activities. Let's look at the pros and cons of holding an event during the school term-time or the school holidays.

■ Holiday clubs

Holiday clubs are often what churches first think of when they want to reach out to children. School holidays can seem very long, children get bored and parents may be very pleased to have them involved and busy at a holiday club. Activities can last all day if we wish, giving us more time to get to know the children. We can include craft work, games and other activities that there may not be time for in a term-time club.

The downside of this is that holiday clubs are often harder work and require more people and preparation than term-time clubs. Some people can't get time off work or need their leave for family holidays. And it is more difficult to make contact with children who have no church friends and to persuade them to come. To sum up, then:

Advantages of a holiday club	Disadvantages of a holiday club
• Because the club is held during the day and in holiday time, more time can be spent with the children, and on crafts and games	• Team members must be able to take time off work to come to the club
• Children who are off school may have nothing to do	• Some children and team members may be on holiday
• The club won't clash with the usual evening clubs, Cubs, Brownies, and so on	• Little or no contact with schools is possible
	• The timing of the club may clash with local authority play schemes

Before you commit yourself to a holiday club, be sure to ask around about holidays and who will be available to help.

■ Term-time clubs

Many churches who have never thought of running a special outreach event during the school term, when they consider the pro and cons, opt for term-time. My experience is that this kind of event often brings in children with no church contact, and publicity is a lot easier. This is especially true if you have already formed good contacts with local schools. Most head teachers are pleased to encourage their children to be involved in community events like this.

A typical term-time club might involve visits to schools during the day and holding the club in the early evening. School visits are important if you want to invite children with no church contact. Schools will usually welcome a visitor to lead an assembly or to show Christian videos, if a proper approach is made to the head teacher (see TaskSheet D). The children can then be invited to the club at the same time. It is even possible to have a club for infants straight after school, and then a later club for juniors after tea, if you can muster enough helpers.

Advantages of term-time clubs:
- You can establish contact with all school-age children through school visits
- Because the club is held in the late afternoon, those with day-time jobs may be able to get there in time to help
- There is a wider availability of dates to choose from in the year

Disadvantages of term-time clubs:
- There is only a short time available to spend with the children each day, and this will restrict what you can put in the programme
- The club may clash with other after-school activities

 Don't assume that all teachers will be free to help with holiday clubs or term-time events. A teacher may be so switched-off from children during the holidays, he or she would hate to be involved in a holiday club. Or a teacher may not be available to help with a club during the term because teaching takes up so much of his or her spare time!

The weekend

Whether during the term or in holiday time, it is a good idea to finish your event with a family service. Scripture Union holiday club publications usually include an outline for a service that follows the holiday club theme.

However, many parents are not used to coming to church and may find a family service too threatening. Inviting them to a family fun evening on the Saturday would be a good way of introducing them to the church and its activities. The programme might include family games, a barn dance, funny sketches or a short video, along with tea or coffee. If you have advertised it as a 'Family Fun Evening', don't 'con' people by preaching at the end of it. I often include puppets, drama or a short video, but avoid a talk.

The venue

Consider carefully the space and facilities you need. If you have a venue that is too small, this may restrict your programme possibilities. You will need to check that:

- your proposed venue fulfils the requirements of the Children Act 1989 (see p 22)
- there is insurance cover and fire safety (see p 23)
- toilets and wash basins are easily reached by young children (a small step may be necessary – Mothercare sell a plastic one)
- you have an adequate First Aid kit and preferably a qualified First Aider on the team. Contact St John's Ambulance Brigade, The British Red Cross Society or St Andrew's Ambulance Association for assistance on First Aid kit contents and courses to train as a First Aider
- strangers cannot easily enter your hall or meeting place
- the heating is adequate
- stone or rough wooden flooring is covered with mats or carpet if children are to sit on the floor
- there is somewhere for the children to put their coats and bags (if you are short of space the children could take them to the area where they meet in their groups)

Scripture Union holiday club programmes usually provide a scheme for the organisation of the venue to suit the requirements of the particular holiday club theme. A reasonably sized

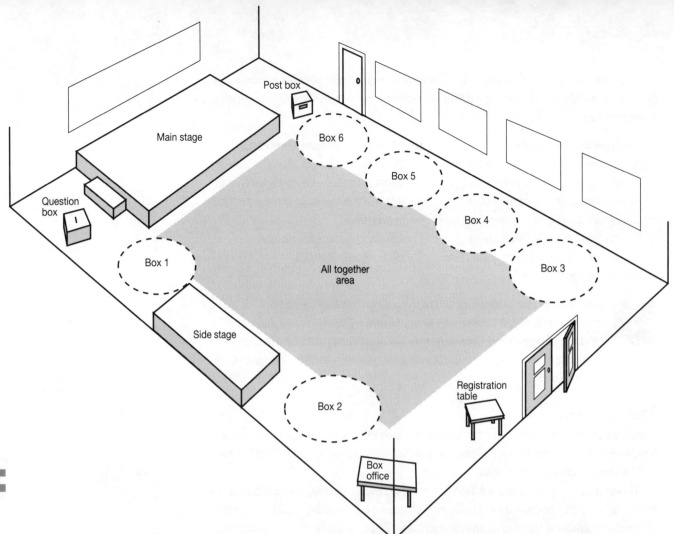

hall can be laid out to accommodate up to a hundred children (a larger number would require more space). Generally there are three basic areas:

- A presentation/stage area for showing videos, staging Bible stories, etc
- A central area where the children sit for the 'all together' times
- The perimeter around the central area where the children meet in their groups

Long group sessions work better when there are plenty of smaller rooms available in which to base the groups.

In general, do consider whether you should use your church premises (the church itself if the chairs move, or the hall) or if another venue, eg a local school or community hall, might be more appropriate. The danger of using a community hall is that the children and parents won't so easily associate the event with your church. One club I knew ran brilliantly off-site, attracting many children, but when it was time to invite them to the church, very few came.

The theme

It is a good idea to choose one theme for the whole event and then aim to tell a Bible story that is linked to this theme each day. It is important to think about the children you hope to attract and to find a theme that will be helpful and attractive to them.

Scripture Union publishes new holiday club material each year, giving Bible stories, crafts, group ideas and lots more, and there is a good choice of themes and approaches in these. However, you may want to think up your own theme and produce your own material. Anyone with time and imagination can do this. I usually start with what I think God wants to say to the children, the message from the Bible I should present. Then I work out how to present it and the visual approach. Other people start with a great visual idea of what the club will look like and work the Bible material into it. Look at other holiday club publications to get ideas and to discover the many ways of communicating the message. And remember the importance of seeking inspiration from God through prayer.

The people

Any church that feels a special outreach event is only for Sunday school children and their leaders will miss an opportunity for God to bless and encourage the whole church. There are many other jobs to do apart from leading groups or the 'all together' sessions (see TaskSheet F). Your programme will rely on as many people in the church as possible providing help. Older teenagers often make great helpers. In fact, no one is too old to take part – children may relate better to 'grandparent'-age team members than to 'parent'-age ones. At a recent event, during the morning service, out of the whole congregation I counted just six people who were not involved! Some church members took time off work (not everyone can); others re-organised their jobs to suit. Such commitment is exciting!

About one adult is needed for every eight children in a term-time club; holiday clubs with crafts need about one adult for every five children. If they can, churches should try to achieve the ratio of one adult to every four children. It is worthwhile considering whether to include leaders from any other children's groups in the area (eg Cubs, Beavers, Brownies, Girls' or Boys' Brigade). These groups might even like to join in, if invited properly in advance.

If there aren't enough people to help with the event, the following problems may arise:

- Children will not get the attention they really need in their groups
- Some children may wander around during group time, instead of joining in
- Registration cards may be badly filled in, leaving an incomplete record for use after the event when you want to invite the children to continue coming
- It will be more difficult to control any 'rowdy' children during the 'all together' time, though it will help if the group leaders sit amongst them at these times (they should do this anyway wherever possible)

■ DIY or specialist?

Many churches are capable of running their own event without outside help. There are many advantages in doing it this way. Local people know the local scene and don't make any obvious mistakes about what is required. Local people stay around after the event is over to continue meeting with the new children that the event may have attracted to the church. And, of course, you don't have to pay a visiting evangelist if you do it yourselves. There is plenty of good holiday club material around with all sorts of ideas, and I hope **Nuts & Bolts** will help, too.

However there are disadvantages to a DIY approach. Some churches may not have a suitable person to lead or share in the leadership of a special outreach event. Others may feel the need for new ideas or a new approach. Some churches don't know how to visit local schools and invite children to come to their club or mission.

You may be able to have the best of both worlds. Some evangelists offer a consultancy service where they help a church to get started on an outreach event but don't actually lead it. See Appendix 1 for further information on inviting an outside evangelist.

■ Training

If people are worried that they may not have the skills to take part, don't panic! In the context of planning a special outreach event, it is worth thinking about providing some measure of training for the whole team: team members may be a bit rusty, some may be having problems in their Sunday school already, others may be completely new to this kind

15

of work. Some may feel that they don't need training as they have looked after children for years. (For this reason I sometimes call training sessions, 'Discussions on working with children'!)

The Scripture Union Training Unit organises a series of courses and produces DIY packs for churches to run their own. If you are inviting an outside evangelist to help or as a consultant, they may be able to give training. But remember that not every evangelist is a good trainer, and some may not have the time to spare unless you book well in advance.

Holiday clubs and missions often have helpers who have no previous experience in children's work, but with adequate preparation they do very well. To give an idea of general training needs, here are some examples of topics on which I am asked to lead sessions:

- The world of a child today
- Helping children become friends with Jesus
- Communicating with children
- Discipline

Working together

I was invited to discuss holding a Bible club in an area where the Methodist church had lots of rooms and a large hall but few children's leaders. The local Anglican church had lots of leaders but no church hall. So they met and, with a little mediation from me and much discussion, they agreed to work together. The club was a great success. I have seen this happen time and time again. It is especially helpful in a small village where no single church could even consider running a holiday club or a regular weekly Bible club on its own.

There can be great advantages in churches working together to run a special outreach event. I have often worked with two churches and sometimes with more than two. There are always a few extra complications, though these are not insurmountable where there is a genuine will to co-operate. Here are some of the extra things to think about:

■ Co-ordinators

It is a good idea for each church involved in the event to have its own event co-ordinator. This ensures that each church is kept informed of its progress and of any needs that arise. The co-ordinators can work together on lists of leaders and helpers and on completing the various tasks.

■ Venue

Where the event is held can make quite a difference, as some people will naturally associate the event with its venue. This may cause tension when there are two or more churches involved. Having the event at a neutral venue, eg in a school, may be a way out of the problem.

■ Final service

If the final service is held at the host church, the other churches involved will have to give up their normal services to take part. I have sometimes tried to solve this by ending missions with a special service in the afternoon. This is usually attended by the children, the most committed church folk and some parents, so perhaps Sunday afternoon is a bad time! I favour using a normal service time, if the other church(es) are able to cancel or have an early service in order to join in.

■ Follow-up

It is sometimes difficult to decide which church to invite children to keep on coming to when the event is over. We don't want children to feel we are competing for them, or to confuse them by inviting them to both or all the churches involved. If a child has any connection at all with one church, invite him to that one. Or if a friend already attends one of the churches, it will be better for him to go with his friend. Much of our work with children depends on our building relationships with them, so, with this in mind, group leaders should invite children in their groups who presently have no church connections to come to their own church.

Other organisations

If there are other meetings going on in the church during the week, it's important to think about how they will affect what you are planning to do. You may have to set up a lot of equipment that won't be easy to pack away each day – though things could be made 'safe' or partly hidden.

Going ahead

To sum up then, before you decide to go ahead with a special outreach event you must be sure about the following:

- God's will – as far as it is possible to determine
- People – are there enough helpers?
- Finance – what can you afford?
- Venue – is it suitable?

17

PLANNING DETAILS

Planning meetings

Having made the decision to go ahead with the special outreach event, you now need to organise at least two or three further planning meetings, maybe more, depending on how much preparation you feel you need. See TaskSheet A for a quick check-list of the tasks that have to be done and the timing for doing them. Use it for reference as you go along.

Three to six months beforehand, your entire outreach team should aim to meet at least once to make final decisions on details such as:

- Target area (geographically)
- Age range
- What to run? When?
- Theme
- Programme
- How many leaders and helpers?
- Prayer strategy
- Publicity
- School visits
- Involvement of children from your own church
- Music
- Finance
- Counselling provision (for team and children) and follow-up strategy
- Training sessions for the team

Make sure that those asked to do particular tasks are invited to the detailed planning meetings. They may have ideas and experience that will be helpful. They will also understand better how their task fits into the whole event.

■ Final briefing

Everyone should attend the last meeting before the event. This will be the time when you distribute sets of 'helpers' notes' and children's funsheets (if you are using them). Discuss the timetable for the event, where team members should be and what they have to do. If anyone who wants to help can't attend this meeting, you should arrange to meet with them another time.

The team

Because a special outreach event involves developing good quality relationships between the children and the team, it is essential to encourage team members to have a real 'heart' for children and to make sure they know how to relate to them. You might find inspiration from particular Bible passages, like Matthew 18:1–14, Psalm 78:1–7 or Deuteronomy 6:4–7. Experienced workers can give advice on how to start talking to children, and what to talk

about (eg people who live at their house, their favourite TV programmes, their friends, their school, etc). You need team members who are sensitive to children and able to pick up any messages they are giving out. This is particularly so for group leaders, where an ability to get to know individual children in their group, to encourage a sense of group togetherness, to draw out the quieter ones as well as listening to the more noisy ones, is essential.

Before getting a team together, it might be useful to draw up a 'job description' listing the qualities you are looking for in your team, and circulate it among possible helpers, giving them plenty of time to pray and consider their response. (But don't make it too hard for people to offer. You will need all the help you can get!) The team can then be formed some six months or so before the event, enabling the members to get to know one another, to explore the material together and to receive any necessary training.

The programme

All Scripture Union holiday club publications have their own suggestions for programmes. You may need to adapt these for your particular situation, but be sure not to miss out any crucial section. Some holiday club themes rely heavily on drama, and the children may miss the whole point if you omit this. If you can't do drama, choose another publication! See TaskSheet E for basic outlines of holiday and term-time club programmes.

Don't be too ambitious with your programme if members of your team have little previous experience or ability. What you can include obviously depends on the skills that you have, so try to bear these in mind as you plan.

■ 'All together' times

If you are inviting an outside evangelist, he or she will probably lead the 'all together' part of the programme. Sometimes, however, the evangelist will want to share out items. A typical 'all together' session might include songs, a time of prayer, a quiz, a memory verse and a Bible story or talk, along with other assorted items from day to day. If you are running your own club or mission, it is not necessary for one person to do all these things. In fact, it gives greater variety and allows people to make full use of their different gifts if you do share them out.

■ Group sessions

The advantage of dividing children into groups by ages is that they are near to each other in ability. The maximum number of children in each group should be eight, though five is better. If there are more than eight children, divide the group into two with a leader or helper for each. It will help then to keep the two groups' funsheets and club cards separate.

It is easiest to count the children during the group times. Some people count them in when they arrive each day with a clicker machine, but children can run in and out of the hall before the start, and others arrive late. They should all have arrived by the time they go to their groups after the 'all together' time.

■ Response to the message

If the aim of our special outreach event is to invite children to respond to the message that we share from the Bible, we must give them the opportunity to do so. It is preferable that this happens when the children are all together rather than at a separate meeting. This gets round some of the practical difficulties of organising another meeting and means that all the children hear what is being said in the context of the overall teaching of the event. A visiting evangelist may have his own preferred method of inviting children to respond.

■ Music

Children usually sing to piano accompaniment in school but guitars are popular, and some children may even be able to play instruments. If you can fit them in, they will enjoy being part of a little music band. If you dare, why not collect or make percussion instruments for them to play? I would suggest that you limit these instruments to a few songs at a particular point in the programme as they can easily be a distraction during prayer, story and drama times.

You will need to work out what songs to use. A visiting evangelist will probably have some favourites or a book to recommend, or might even play an instrument and be happy to teach new songs. Be careful to choose songs that children can easily understand, that will mean something to them when they sing them to themselves after the event. A visit to a Christian bookshop will show you the range of children's songbooks. Here are some song suggestions:

- From **Junior Praise** (Marshall Pickering, an imprint of HarperCollins Publishers) – 'Big man', 'Come on, let's get up and go', 'Get up out of bed', 'Have you seen the pussycat?', 'My God is so big'
- From **The Big Book of Spring Harvest Kids Praise** (International Christian Communications [ICC]) – 'Jesus is greater than the greatest heroes', 'God loves you, and I love you' (also in **Junior Praise**)
- Others – 'For God so loved the world' (**Spring Harvest Kids Praise 1994**, ICC); 'God is good' (**Songs of Fellowship**, Kingsway Music, and **Junior Praise**); 'Take my hand and follow me' (**Sound of Living Waters**, Hodder & Stoughton)

The team could learn your chosen songs in advance. Don't rely too heavily on a visitor for music, or what will happen after the event is over? Some churches solve the problem by using taped music. Scripture Union produces cassettes to accompany **The Light Factory** and **Newshounds**. They are worth investigating, even if you are not following those particular holiday club programmes.

Remember that you may need written permission from publishers if you are planning to write up the words of songs on paper or an overhead projector. The words of many songs and hymns are covered by the Church Copyright Licence for local church reproduction. For a small annual fee, based on the size of the main congregation, the licence permits the church to reproduce these words onto OHP acetates, in service bulletins, songsheets, songbooks produced by the church for its own use, and so on. Full details can be obtained from Christian Copyright Licensing Limited (see Appendix 2).

Publicity

Letters home that don't arrive. Invitation cards that get screwed up. Words that go in one ear and out the other. Have you got any kids like this in your Sunday group? I have often visited a church for a special outreach event to discover at the end that some people – adults *and* children who attend the church regularly – didn't know about it. You need to get people so involved in the event, they can't possibly forget.

There is no point in putting on the event unless the right children hear about it. And there is little chance that putting up a few posters will have them turning up in droves! You have to go out and persuade them to come. But publicity can be very expensive, so you want to make the best use of it. To produce your own is hard work and requires some expertise and, as your main publicity will be seen by so many people, it must be good quality or it will reflect on the event and the church. TaskSheet C gives fuller notes on publicity.

I know that the Bible says the *people* are the church not the building, but the building does matter to visitors. If it looks awful, people will think that it reflects our attitude to God. Many churches never think about how their church looks to a non-churchgoer, and some modern churches don't look much like churches at all. TaskSheet C also has ideas for making your church building a good advertisement for your planned event.

Dedication service

You might consider having a special service of dedication for the event before it starts. This could include a short explanation of what is happening in case others in the church aren't sure, perhaps a talk on Jesus and children (Matthew 18 & 19) and a prayer of dedication for all those taking part.

Setting up

Be sure you allow enough time and get enough volunteers to set up all the equipment needed for the first day of your event. You will have a lot of fun decorating the venue. Posters, bunting, banners – any of these can brighten up a hall and make it special. A visiting evangelist may bring his or her own decorations.

It is usually better for children to sit on the floor for the 'all together' time. If you can get some carpet, this will define the area you want them in, and make it more comfortable. Of course, not all adults find it easy to sit on the floor, so be considerate and don't exclude anyone in this way.

Group times may be better on the floor too. If the children are sitting on carpet, they will need 'press on' boards for their funsheets. Younger or older age groups may benefit from being in a room by themselves or with one other group. If your event has longer group times, and there is space, the children will enjoy making 'dens' all around the building.

Equipment

There may be a lot of equipment to collect together. A check-list is given on TaskSheet A.

■ Folders

It is a good idea to provide a folder or box for each group, which contains pencils, crayons, club cards, funsheets, sticky name badges and anything else required for the day. Club cards and funsheets can be kept in the folder or box each night. If you need to ask someone to stand in for a leader who cannot come for that session, just give them the folder and they will have all they need for their group.

■ Video

Showing a video to small groups is an easy and straightforward operation (provided you have a video player and a television set of course!). However, showing to a large audience is more complicated and can be expensive. You may like to consider using either a video projector onto a large screen, or a number of monitors or television sets spread around your audience. The first way works well, and modern LCD video projectors are easy to set up, but they do need effective blackout, and they are expensive to hire.

If you opt for the multi-set showing, it is important to understand the difference between monitors and televisions, to establish what connections and sockets they require, and to know how much cable you have to run round all the sets in such a way that people will not trip over them. The sets must be mounted on sturdy, safe stands high enough for everyone to see them clearly. Be sure to find someone in the church who knows what they are doing when setting up this kind of viewing, or contact a specialist video equipment supplier in **Yellow Pages**.

Write to Scripture Union's Sound and Vision Unit for more information about setting up video equipment. They will also send a catalogue of videos produced by Scripture Union, which you can show during your special outreach event or at the family fun times.

■ Prizes

Prizes are not necessary, but they can be an incentive for children to join in. If you decide to award prizes, you will have to devise a prize scheme. My suggestion is to give points (eg rubber stamp 'splodges' stamped onto the back of club cards) for answering quiz questions, saying memory verses, and so on. If you do this, the children need to have their club cards right from the start of the meeting each night. Any child who comes later, after the first day of the event, can be given a club card with their first splodge already on it. During the 'all together' times, children should collect their points from the group leaders nearest to them, as directed by the 'up front' leader. Award points during group times, but be sure to be fair across the groups. At the end of the week collect the club cards and award prizes according to number of points. I award lots of first and second prizes (usually books), and then have a specially printed 'runners-up' puzzle book for everyone else.

■ Bookstall and badges

If you are going to have a bookstall, make sure it is well stocked with children's and family books. Someone should be given the job of looking after the bookstall and clearing up each night. A visiting evangelist may organise his or her own bookstall.

Badge-making machines are very popular. They are quite simple to work, but it is better if only one or two people are in charge of them. The children choose a design (or make their own) and then the badge is made up while they wait. Badge machines can be hired from play resource centres or local education/teachers' centres (or a local evangelist may have one). The bookstall and the badge machine need a strong table each, preferably about six feet long.

The Children Act 1989

You must register with your local authority if the following details apply:
- Children under 8 are involved in an activity without their parents being present
- The activity lasts longer than two hours, with the children present (ie not including preparation time)
- The activity runs for six days or more in any one year (those running less than six days who come into the first two categories must inform the social services, but need not register)

What do they check?
- Leadership must be fit, trained and experienced
- Ratio of adults to children – one adult to eight children is suggested
- Records must be kept of children attending, team and anyone else employed on the premises
- The venue must be safe, bright and welcoming (there are laid-down requirements for space per child, kitchen facilities, number of toilets and washbasins)
- The activities must be varied, suitable to the ages and must not discriminate against sex, race or religion

If you suspect that registration is necessary, write to your local authority social services department, giving full details of your planned activity. There is an outline for such a letter on p 27.

Even if you are not required to register, you should inform your local authority that

you are running the event. Some local authorities have already indicated that they do not require holiday clubs or beach-mission-type activities to register. This is because our aim in running them is not 'day care', which is covered by the Act. While we do 'care for' children in our activities, this is not our main purpose.

If the Children Act worries you, remember that local authorities have to deal with much more difficult problems than church activities. Many will be delighted that the church is running something for children in the area. The Children Act is a great piece of legislation for children. It encourages us all to improve the standards of care within our children's clubs, and gives us 'legal clout' for proper training and better facilities for children in our churches.

Special needs

Be aware of and prepared for children who have special needs. Although it is best to get to know such children well beforehand – their likes and dislikes, their favourite places – this may be impossible if it is their first visit to church. Check if they have friends in the church. Is there anything they may be afraid of? How far can they walk happily? Discuss all the options with their parents.

Think carefully how suitable your venue is, eg toilet facilities and access for wheel chairs. Are there people on your team who are able to cope with special needs?

Special needs that I have encountered in working with children over the years include deafness, speech problems, confinement to a wheelchair or special buggy, intellectual impairment, plus a whole range of special medical needs such as epilepsy, asthma, allergies to nuts, biscuits, additives in orange squash, and so on. Many children with special needs just want to be accepted and treated as normally as possible.

First Aid

Check that you have all you need in your First Aid kit, and make it clear to everyone where it is stored. There should be someone present each day who knows how to use it. Everyone should know which team member has First Aid or medical training, just in case.

Insurance

Check that your church insurance covers you for public liability in connection with having a special outreach event. It is worth making sure that you are covered regarding the age range of the children coming and the activities you plan to hold. Be especially careful if there are plans to go away from church premises. If you have a local authority licence for the premises, please make sure that you know the details of this licence.

Fire safety

Check that all fire exits and extinguishers are in working order. You also need some way of attracting attention in an emergency. If you don't have a proper alarm system, perhaps six quick blasts on a whistle will serve. On hearing the alarm, there should be instant silence while everyone waits for further instructions. It may not be practical to have a full fire drill, but team members must know how to react in an emergency. This means that the alarm should not be used for any other purpose during the event.

If children are to be scattered all around the premises during the event, you need some way of checking that they have all evacuated the building should this be necessary. Group leaders could have an attendance card (see p 26) for their group, small enough to fit in their pocket, on which they tick-off the children as they arrive each day.

Road safety

We must be careful that children walking to and from the event can cross nearby roads safely. It is a good idea to appoint someone with the responsibility of patrolling road crossings. They could wear bright yellow jackets to help with identification. If the road is very busy and traffic congestion is likely to be a problem as parents drop or collect their children, we should inform the police. I have always found them willing to assist with this sort of special activity.

It will be helpful if team members park so as to allow plenty of space for parents to get as near the church as possible when they drop their children off. In particular, team members should avoid parking directly outside the door used by children, to make crossing the road safer. You may be able to borrow cones for this purpose.

Child safety

The safety of the children who come to your holiday club or mission should be paramount. At the end of each day you must ensure that they are collected by their parents, unless their parents have told you that someone else will be coming to collect them, or if children are old enough to go home on their own and have been given permission by their parents to do so. Remember, if there is someone different coming for a child, to establish who that person is. Then if Mum or Dad should turn up later, you know with whom the child has gone.

Be careful that no one who shouldn't comes in and takes a child. An intruder is less likely to come right inside a church, so this is one good reason for finishing the event with the children in their small groups – they can stay with their group leader until someone collects them.

It should be emphasised that team members must be properly vetted and judged to be fit and proper persons to work with children. It is a good idea to ask for a letter of reference from volunteers whose background is not known, perhaps from a trustworthy minister or church leader who knows them well. Sadly, concerns may also arise over a child being alone with a team member in a separate room or an enclosed area. When you are considering your venue and programme, please make these concerns part of your thinking. For children to be taken advantage of in any context is bad enough; for this to happen within a Christian setting is disastrous.

Storing information

Registering the children is very important but can cause problems. One club in Liverpool registered 125 children on the door as they arrived and it took over twenty minutes to get them all in! And this was with six helpers doing the registering. It led to major problems with programme timing as we were only running quite a short club each day. Since then, I have registered children in their groups as soon as they arrive.

The team members welcoming the children as they arrive should therefore direct them and their parents (or the adults who bring them) to their groups straight away, so that the adults can fill in the club cards (ie registration cards) for the children before they go. This helps to get the information correct and makes it safer for children, as the grown-ups hand them over to the group leaders who are responsible for them during the event. Group leaders can then ensure that the children leave with the appropriate person at the end.

There are sample club cards on p 26 showing the information you should keep to satisfy the Children Act 1989 (see above). If the children keep their cards during the event (for prize points), make sure they hand them in to their group leaders before they go, or cards may get lost.

Information on children could be stored on a computer, which would let you print out follow-up visiting lists easily. If you input more than just a name and address, your

computer must be registered under The Data Protection Act 1984. Guidance Notes on the Act are available from: The Information Services Department, Data Protection Registrar, Wycliffe House, Water Lane, Wilmslow, Cheshire, SK19 5AF; telephone (01625) 535777, fax no. (01625) 524510.

Follow-up

About three months after a club week, the vicar phoned me. 'We didn't get many children carrying on coming after that mission you did, Steve.'

'Oh, I'm sorry to hear that. What did you do afterwards?'

'Do? We didn't do anything,' he replied.

And that was the problem. Happily, in that situation it wasn't too late to go back into the local schools to invite the children to a club reunion. Many of the same children came again, and this time the church was ready to visit them and invite them to a series of clubs designed to follow-on from the special event.

So, as part of the planning for the event, think through what you will do afterwards (see TaskSheet G). This may be the opportunity to absorb into your usual programme any new ideas that were introduced during the event. Not everything that works for a special event will work forever, but you will probably get inspiration. Check at this time too that the materials you are using with the children are still suitable.

Every child who comes to the special outreach event should receive a visit and a personal invitation to church activities, and ideally the visit should take place in the week after the event while it is still fresh in people's minds. Visits can be poorly done or neglected, partly because everyone has been so busy and the natural reaction when it is all over is to have a rest! However the long-term effectiveness of the event can be spoilt as a result. Plan to do visits now so that you are ready when the time comes.

■ **EXAMPLES OF CLUB CARD, REGISTRATION/RECORD CARD AND ATTENDANCE CARD, FOR USE OR ADAPTATION.**

Club Card

(Event logo)

Name _____ Leader _____

Address _____

_____

Age _____ Birthday _____ Phone _____

I go to Sunday School / a church club ☐ Yes ☐ No Where _____

Parent/Guardian _____

Special Needs _____

Registration Form

Name

Telephone

Age

Attendance | DAY 1 | DAY 2 | DAY 3 | DAY 4 | DAY 5

Age group

I am a member of

group

Anything special the leaders should know?

Record Card

Name

Age   Birthday

Group

Home Address

Tel.

Parents' Names

Friend with whom you came

How did you hear about (name)?
(Which church, school, friend, etc?)

Other details (health, etc.)

Group Attendance Card

Please carry at all times in case of EMERGENCY

Age ☐   (Logo)

Name	M	T	W	T	F	S

Social Services Department
(Address)

Dear Sir,

I am writing on behalf of our church to inform you of a holiday club for children that we plan to run during the Easter school holidays in 19XX. I hope to include sufficient information for you to decide whether you require us to register under the Children Act 1989.

At present we plan to run the holiday club from **(day)** to **(day)** on **(date/month)**. We shall meet each morning from **(time)** to **(time)**. We intend to invite children aged **(age range)**. There will be no charge for this activity as the church considers it part of our ministry to the community. **(Or charge details, if you are charging.)**

Our purpose in running this activity is not primarily 'day care'. We want to share stories from the Bible with all who come, for example giving those who don't usually come to church the opportunity to discover for themselves some of the great things Jesus did. We shall be following The **J Team** material from Scripture Union whose advice we have sought in planning this holiday club. This material involves a great variety of activities including songs, videos, stories, crafts, games, puzzle sheets and discussion. At least half of the time will be spent in small groups which will stay roughly the same from day to day.

We are building a team of people to lead the holiday club. They vary greatly in age, skills and training, but include qualified teachers and experienced Sunday School leaders. We shall be organising training sessions for the whole team nearer the time. In an activity like this, to which all are invited, we cannot be sure how many children will come, but we are aiming to have one team member for every five children. We shall have registration cards for each child, preferably to be filled in by their parents.

The holiday club will meet in our church which, whilst being quite old, is well maintained and safe. We shall decorate our hall with bright posters, banners and bunting. We have good kitchen facilities to prepare refreshments for the children. We have adequate toilet facilities with washbasins for the number we are expecting.

We hope that our plans meet with your approval and await your consideration regarding the Children Act and possible registration under the Act.

Yours sincerely

(Name)

DURING THE EVENT

Prayer first

Encourage all the team to arrive in plenty of time, at least half-an-hour before the programme begins each day, to take part in the team prayer sessions. They will then be spiritually, mentally and physically prepared for the arrival of the children. Try to start this prayer time promptly and allow late-comers to join in.

■ **Pray that:**
- **children will come**
- **parents will be happy to bring them**
- **everyone will feel welcome**
- **children will enjoy the club**
- **team members will be able to respond to the children well**
- **God will keep everyone safe**

Last-minute reminders

Take two minutes after your prayer time to remind everyone of the programme. There is always someone who is not sure what's happening. Supply sticky badges for everyone on the team, with a space on each badge for their name – a great help, especially for a visiting evangelist. Children and parents who are new to the church will also find it easier to remember names if the team wear badges.

Prayer during

If you have a prayer time in your groups during the event, leaders will find it easier if you all stop and pray at the same time. This is particularly true if the groups are all in one room. It also helps to remind the group leaders to pray with the children. I suggest a few minutes are allocated and everyone is only allowed to whisper during that time.

Some children may be used to praying, others will never ever have prayed seriously. To get them started, group leaders will have to show them what to do. To those children who don't know how to pray, leaders can simply explain that prayer is talking to a very special friend – Jesus – who hears us even though we can't see him. Group leaders can ask the children for ideas, needs or suggestions for prayer. Some children prefer to write down a prayer before saying it. I have a large 'rainbow' on which I invite children to stick their written prayers. We then use these prayers during the event.

Discipline

This is always important, but especially so when you are inviting children who don't usually come to church. Most will be no problem at all, but there may be some who just don't know how to behave in church activities (or anywhere for that matter!).

Agree beforehand your policy on behaviour, and stick to it. You may have to explain to anyone who misbehaves that you won't let them spoil the club for others. Perhaps you could warn them once and, if they continue to misbehave, do what you said you would do. This usually means that they go and sit at the back next to a team helper (an adult) or that they leave the room for five minutes. In the latter case, an adult must go with them to check they do what they are told (but see p 24 'Child safety'). Under no circumstances hit a child. Only ever use physical restraint to stop children injuring themselves.

Sometimes children misbehave because we ask them to do things that they can't do. Some may have special needs, which makes it difficult for them to join in fully. Be aware of these possibilities and handle them as carefully as you can. It obviously helps if you can build up a friendship with their parents and discover how best to help children like this.

Occasionally behaviour problems are caused by a poor programme. If the children are sitting around waiting for things to happen, or there is too much talking up front, or they can't understand what is being said, they will get restless. Children are not as polite as adults! Try to make sure that your programme is good, well-prepared and understandable.

During an 'all together' time I often like to listen to individual children saying memory verses, for example, or suggesting things for prayer. Once, however, this activity led the others to chatter and mess about, so I had to change the programme for that particular event. If certain items on the programme allow or even provoke bad behaviour, learn from the problem and adapt the programme next time. If you anticipate problems, plan to have activities ready for the children to come into at the start, preferably sitting at tables. Be aware that some will mess about because they can't write or work out puzzles. Provide them with alternatives (eg colouring or doing simpler funsheets). Playing quiet classical music can also help to calm children down.

In all cases of discipline, we must remember that 95% of children behave well and don't cause a problem. It is not fair to them if we let one or two children spoil the event for everyone. My guiding principle is to be firm and fair.

Prayer after

When all the children and parents have gone, get leaders and helpers together for a brief chat and prayer. This is a chance to review the programme, consider any changes and share problems. Some leaders may have difficult children. Some may have very bright children or children with learning difficulties. They may be able to get ideas from the others that will help in those situations. And, of course, you can pray over them all. If we asked God to bring children and that they would enjoy the event, we should thank him if he has answered our prayers.

As most people will be getting tired by this time, and some will need to go, keep this prayer time short. (If you don't, some people won't stay to pray another day.)

Family events

■ Fun?

For me family fun events began after only one parent turned up to my first family service! Other parents seemed unwilling to come to 'church' for their first visit to us. So we began to organise events that were mostly fun, games and food. After coming to these and discovering that Christians were quite safe really, many were willing to come to 'church proper'.

■ Assorted fun

A variety of activities will help to cater for the wide range of people and ages present. The whole event usually lasts for about 90 minutes. The following may be included:

- **Parachute games** – borrow a parachute from your nearest play resource centre, or see Appendix 2
- **Mad, dashing-about games for children**, eg Musical Islands, Captain's Orders, Musical Numbers. There are many excellent games in **Over 300 Games for All Occasions** by Patrick Goodland (Scripture Union). Or there is **The Great Play Times Games Kit**, available from The National Playing Fields Association, 25 Ovington Square, London, SW3 1LQ, which contains a card index full of games in various sections
- **A barn dance** – this is a great way of getting people to mix. Children could dance with a grown-up. (That'll get the adults up!) Use simple dances like the Pat-a-cake Polka, Circassian Circle, Farmer's Jig, Cumberland Reel or even the Hokey Cokey. Make sure you have a good, clear caller and adequate amplification. For books and tapes on barn dancing, contact The English Folk Dance and Song Society, Cecil Sharp House, 2 Regents Park Road, London, NW1 7AY, telephone 0171 284 0534
- **Family group games** – divide people into four large groups. Not everyone needs to take part; some can just support the others. Play games like Chinese Laundry, the 'Bring Me' game, Give Us A Clue, Guess the TV Theme, Singing Nursery Rhymes, Pictionary and Newspaper Hunt for Headlines
- **A puppet play, drama or short video** – this is the only 'spiritual' input that you would have in the event

■ Potted sports

This is when you set up games right around the room, and families play them all for a score out of 10. A small prize is given to the winning family. The games should be short and simple, eg tin-can shy, building a house of cards, Bagatelle, covering a penny in a bucket of water, and so on. For full details of this idea, see **Family Evangelism** by John Hattam (Scripture Union).

Why not invite dads to run the games during a family fun evening? This gets the men involved in a way that makes them feel part of what's happening.

■ Other options

Many other activities are possible. We have tried picnics, hiring a sports centre and a swimming pool, films, banner-making, suppers and all kinds of outings.

■ Just a social?

A friend of mine ran a family fun event in a church once a month for a few months. After the third or fourth event, a father came to him and asked, 'Where's the catch?' He had come to the first assuming that he would be preached at. If he had been, it would have confirmed his belief that the church was out to get him, to 'con' him even. My friend hadn't preached at the fun evenings, and eventually the father started coming to family services too, when there certainly was preaching.

Be careful not to try and fool people by preaching at events billed as fun and games. They will soon learn and vote with their feet. Besides, the main aim of these sorts of events is to get to know people, and for them to see that church members are normal (well, reasonably normal) people who happen to believe in the Lord Jesus Christ. This puts a great emphasis on church members not hiding in the kitchen or being too busy to talk to visitors during family fun times.

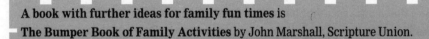

A book with further ideas for family fun times is
The Bumper Book of Family Activities by John Marshall, Scripture Union.

Family service

Many events finish with a special family service. This should involve as many people as possible from the event. If you are having a visiting evangelist, be sure that some leaders from the church are also there, so that when parents come again they recognise someone 'up front'. Children could share in the Bible reading or prayers. The service could include their favourite songs from the event, a quiz on all the stories, asking children to say any memory verses they have learnt, and generally explaining the event to those present – visitors and regulars – who may not have been involved. If you are having prizes, why not save them for this service? This will provide an extra incentive to come.

Most churches where I have done holiday clubs have arranged a display of crafts for one of the family events. One church had a keen photographer in the congregation, who took photos all week and created an excellent display of them for the family service. At another church, the children had written such lovely prayers for my 'prayer and praise' rainbow that we used them in the service.

AFTER THE EVENT

How many children will carry on coming?

This is very difficult to estimate, but experience shows that it will depend a lot on your follow-up visiting and the activities your church can offer to children (see TaskSheet G). The questionnaire on TaskSheet G.3, for use in follow-up visiting, allows you the opportunity to discover what sort of activity they might come to. You may be able to adjust your church's programme to suit. Make sure that the children's activities run by the church after the event are the best you can make them.

Scripture Union publishes the Sharing and Learning Together (SALT) programme each quarter for use in church Sunday groups or midweek clubs for children. Contact the Scripture Union Marketing Department for sample material if you haven't seen the new-look SALT, which has full colour leaflets for children and a fully integrated scheme across the age ranges including family services and sermon notes.

More people in general?

Check that your church is prepared for the hoped-for increase in children coming – you may need extra helpers. Some members of the outreach team may agree to help for a few weeks after the special event, even if they can't commit themselves to helping long term.

Assessment

A little while after the special outreach event is over, it is useful to get together and reflect on what you have done. Look back at your aims and see how well you achieved them. Be honest. So many churches put poor attendance or failure to achieve aims as down to the Lord having different ideas. Maybe he did, but don't make this just an excuse. Are your original aims still valid? Would you approach matters in a different way next time? Of course there may have been factors beyond your control. (See also p 10, 'Previous missions'.)

While the event is still fresh in your minds, write down some of your conclusions for the future. You may wish to avoid making the same mistakes, or to build on successes. Above all, don't give up just because it didn't quite work out this time.

■ Assess the visiting evangelist

If you had a visiting evangelist, discuss his contribution. What did he bring to the event? Could you have done just as well? Would you have him again? If not, could you tell him why not? (But give him a chance to recover from the event first!) Some evangelists have assessment questionnaires that they ask churches to fill in and send confidentially to their advisors. This is one of the few ways evangelists have of getting an objective assessment of their work.

Reunion

It may be helpful to run a 'Reunion' weekend or one-night party for all the children who came to the special outreach event. Send out invitations perhaps, and follow the theme used in the event. A reunion is a helpful way of getting in touch with children who haven't been to regular activities for a while, and if a family activity went well during the event, consider running another one as part of the reunion.

TASKSHEETS

The following pages detail various tasks relating to a special outreach event. You may decide that they are not all necessary. The event co-ordinator should make sure that the tasks you do want are undertaken. You may photocopy these TaskSheets to give to the people doing the tasks.

If you are having a visiting evangelist, he or she may be able to offer advice on these tasks, so please check. There are always different ways of doing things.

Artwork

Some of the TaskSheets include artwork which you will need to modify in order to use. If someone has a computer in your church, you may be able to create something from scratch, using this book for ideas only. Or you could print out the wording that you want to use and paste it onto artwork from **Nuts & Bolts**. Be careful to produce attractive material – computers can give you boring stuff just as easily as good. Try to include some illustration on each poster or leaflet.

Printing

Why not print straight from the computer for small quantities and use a local high street printer for larger numbers? Items for the general public need to be of high quality, so be sure that your computer printer is good enough. (Dot matrix printers rarely are; ink jets and lasers are usually OK.) Some photocopiers don't produce good enough quality copies to offer as publicity to the public, so be careful. They are fine for internal use.

CPO (see Appendix 2) offers good quality, full colour publicity for use by churches and Christian groups. They have an extensive range of materials available, from invitations to welcome materials, bookmarks, posters and leaflets to introduce your church. They can also give helpful advice to churches about producing their own publicity.

There are other good Christian print services around. You could consult **The UK Christian Handbook** to find out about these, or why not ask other churches in your area to recommend anyone they know?

CHECK-LISTS

COUNTDOWN CHECK-LIST

12–9 months before the event

☐ Consider why you want to have a special outreach event and make the decision to run it.

☐ Confirm the dates with your own and other local church leaders (especially if it is a joint-church event. It is courteous to inform other churches in any case).

☐ Set in motion the means of financing it.

☐ Decide on the venue and book it, checking for safety and public liability insurance requirements.

☐ Are the event and the venue in line with the Children Act 1989?

☐ If you are going to do so, book a visiting evangelist. Some evangelists get booked up much further in advance than this, so please check.

8–6 months before

☐ Inform the whole church that you are planning to hold the event.

☐ Appoint the following people who can begin planning their tasks, using the appropriate TaskSheets for guidance:

- the event co-ordinator
- the prayer organiser
- someone to liaise with local schools
- the follow-up organiser

☐ Organise the church to pray.

☐ Contact individuals in the church who have the potential to be on the team, and invite them to take part.

☐ Set the planning meeting dates.

3–2 months before

☐ Decide the target area, age range and the theme of your special outreach event.

☐ Discuss the programme details, dates and times with everyone involved.

☐ Try to identify what skills need to be developed in the team and organise any necessary training.

☐ Appoint a publicity officer and decide how you want to publicise the event.

☐ Write to CPO (see Appendix 2) to find out what publicity they can offer.

☐ Make contact with local schools.

☐ Invite local groups, eg the Cubs, Brownies, Girls' and Boys' Brigades, to join in.

☐ Make sure that anyone who is a regular user of your venue is aware of the dates and times of your event.

CHECK-LISTS

6 weeks before

☐ Finalise group leaders and helpers.

☐ Distribute the group material (funsheets, etc) to each of the leaders so that they can begin familiarising themselves with it.

☐ Hold any training that you have decided is suitable.

☐ Musicians and actors begin rehearsing and learning their parts.

☐ Remind the children who might be coming, and their parents, that the event will take place. Invite adults to book dates and times in their diaries.

☐ Make arrangements for hiring or borrowing any technical or electronic equipment that is required.

☐ List the resources that are needed, eg pens, paper, catering requirements.

☐ Appoint a team of people to plan and organise the catering.

☐ If you are going to have one, begin planning items for the family fun time.

4 weeks before

☐ Advertise the event beyond the local congregation.

☐ Meet with team leaders to pray and discuss any last-minute requirements.

☐ Collect all the resources that you need.

1 day before

☐ Move into the hall and prepare the furniture and displays, setting up as much equipment as possible.

☐ Finish preparing craft work and photocopying funsheets, quiz sheets, etc.

1 hour before

☐ The team arrives for Bible study and prayer before the event begins.

CHECK-LISTS

EQUIPMENT CHECK-LIST

'All together' time

☐ Songs on acetate or cards

☐ OHP and screen or easel

☐ Music and instruments

☐ Visual aids

☐ Quizzes and quiz sheets

☐ Memory verses

Group times

☐ Funsheets

☐ Pencils, crayons, pens

☐ Rubbers, sharpeners

☐ Club/registration cards for each child

☐ Attendance cards for each group

☐ Bibles

☐ 'Press on' boards

☐ Large-size numeral or title for each group

Hall

☐ Banners

☐ Bunting

☐ Posters on event theme

☐ Carpet to sit on

☐ Tape recorder

☐ Video and video equipment

Displays

☐ Bookstall

☐ Bible reading notes display

☐ Badge machine

☐ Tables for all the above

Outside the church

☐ Poster or banner

☐ Welcome signs

☐ Direction signs if needed

☐ Parking cones, signs if needed

Refreshments

☐ Paper napkins, plates, crockery, cups

☐ Tea or coffee

☐ Squash

☐ Biscuits

Other

☐ Invitation cards

☐ Colouring competition sheets

☐ Response cards

☐ Prayer bookmarks

PRAYER

6–8 MONTHS BEFORE, ORGANISE THE WHOLE CHURCH TO PRAY

☐ Give out a prayer card as a helpful reminder.

☐ Encourage church members to stop whatever they are doing at certain times of the day for prayer.

☐ Arrange for someone to pray for each leader in the team throughout the planning stages and during the event itself.

☐ Write regular bulletins for church notices or magazine to update people from time to time on specific prayer requests and answers.

PRODUCE PRAYER BOOKMARKS

☐ Give everyone in the church a bookmark each to remind them to pray.

☐ Give two or three bookmarks to each person helping with the event. Encourage them to find two people who will pray for them, and thus build a team of prayer support.

ORGANISE PRAYER TRIPLETS

☐ Print a special card with space for people to write the names of those they are praying for in their triplet. Each of the three may nominate three others they wish to pray for, so the group prays for nine people.

INVOLVE THE CHILDREN

☐ Give the children in your Sunday school a prayer card or bookmark to encourage them to pray that their friends will come to the event. Introduce the card a few weeks before, in the context of some teaching about prayer. This ensures that the children in the church know about the event and invite their friends (see TaskSheet C, 'Invitation cards').

ORGANISE THE TEAM PRAYER SESSIONS

☐ Ask team members to arrive at least half an hour before the programme begins each day for prayer sessions, and start these promptly.

☐ Themes for team prayer should arise from the overall theme of the event. Scripture Union holiday club publications contain suggested outlines for these sessions.

☐ Meet together again after the programme ends each day for a brief chat and prayer for the day's activities and for the children.

■ **THE PRAYER CARDS AND BOOKMARKS ON THE NEXT TWO PAGES CAN BE ADAPTED TO SUIT YOUR NEEDS**

This card belongs to ....

My friends are ....

I am praying that
my friends will come to ....

(Event name/logo)

(Event name/logo)

(Event dates)

Remember to pray for

_____
_____
_____
_____

Please Pray

**Remember these events
at our Family Fun Day**

(Event logo)

(Event venue & dates)

PRAYER TRIPLETS

_____

_____

*And pray in the Spirit on
all occasions with all kinds
of prayers and requests.
With this in mind,
be alert and always
keep on praying
for all the saints.*

Ephesians 6:18

I am praying for

_____

_____

Pray
- **Daily**
- **Confidently**
- **Thankfully**

Be strong in the Lord

(Event venue & dates)

This card belongs to

I am praying that my friends will come to

(Name/logo of event)

(Dates)

Pray always. 'Pray for one another'
James 5:16

1.

2.

3.

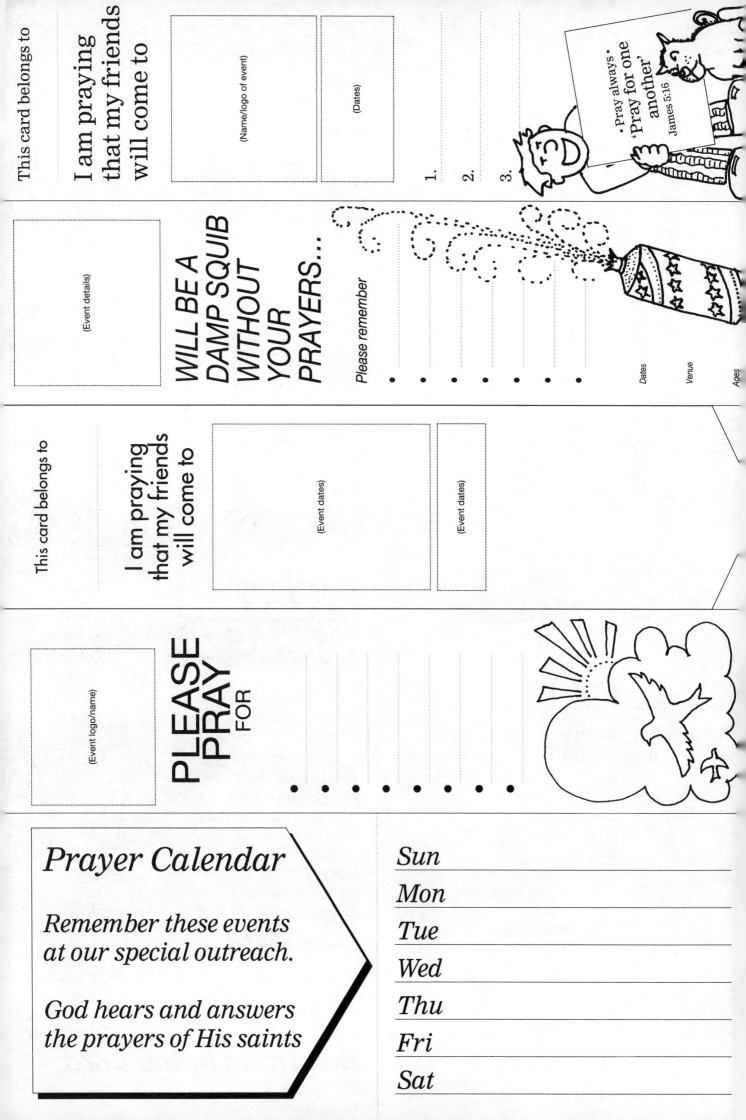

(Event details)

WILL BE A DAMP SQUIB WITHOUT YOUR PRAYERS...

Please remember

• • • • • • •

Dates

Venue

Ages

This card belongs to

I am praying that my friends will come to

(Event dates)

(Event dates)

(Event logo/name)

PLEASE PRAY FOR

• • • • • • • •

Prayer Calendar

Remember these events at our special outreach.

God hears and answers the prayers of His saints

Sun

Mon

Tue

Wed

Thu

Fri

Sat

PUBLICITY

6–8 MONTHS BEFORE, INFORM THE WHOLE CHURCH

☐ Liaise with the prayer organiser in the production of prayer cards and bookmarks (see B.2 and B.3).

☐ Make regular use of the church's usual methods of communication, eg church bulletins, noticeboards and the magazine.

☐ So that children in the church realise the purpose of the event, tell them well in advance. Use a whole lesson in your Sunday school times. Perhaps you could take the story of how Jesus told his disciples to 'Go into all the world…' (Matthew 28:16-20). Explain that the special outreach event is one way of doing this.

☐ If you are still not sure that the children in your Sunday school will come, try a special offer! Give them all a special token worth a free metal badge when they come to the club! Or perhaps a prize for bringing a friend.

PRODUCE INVITATION CARDS

☐ These can be simple A6 or folded A5 cards. Only include essential information – time, date and place. An enquiry phone number is also useful.

☐ Print a brief notice about any family events on the invitation card so that parents know about them.

☐ Include any necessary safety advice on the invitation.

☐ Get the children in your Sunday school to make personal invitations for one of their friends who doesn't yet come to regular church activities. Provide appropriate cards, stencils of designs, and sticky shapes. Write out the wording with the details for them to copy. If you are using sticky badges for the club, stick one of those on each invitation.

☐ Or you could print an invitation, like a children's party invitation, for the children to fill in the blanks and give to a friend.

PRODUCE POSTERS

☐ Have enough posters for each school and for the church. The bigger the better outside the church. Schools and shops may not be able to display very large posters, so have some A3 or A4 ones as well.

☐ Put only the essential details on the posters – the event title, place, time and dates.

☐ If you only want a few posters, it may be more economic to hand-write them. Make sure that the lettering is very thick and clearly visible from a distance.

☐ Or simply enlarge the invitation card on a photocopier. If the card is designed on a computer, A4 posters can be produced in the same way.

MAKE A BANNER

☐ Display a banner about the event outside the church. Planning permission is not usually necessary for less than a week's use.

☐ If you are inviting a visiting evangelist, he or she may already have a suitable banner.

PUBLICITY

WRITE TO CPO

☐ Their address: CPO, Garcia Estate, Canterbury Road, Worthing, Sussex, BN13 1BW, telephone (01903) 264556. They will send a catalogue and samples of their bright and colourful children's invitation cards. CPO will overprint these at very reasonable cost with the details you supply.

☐ Not all CPO designs for invitation cards have matching posters, so check first.

☐ CPO will provide poster 'blanks' for churches to adapt for their own use.

USE A LOGO

☐ If your church has a logo, include it on the publicity. Some Scripture Union holiday clubs have a logo you may use, or you may design one specially. A logo will help people to associate the event's publicity items with each other.

☐ Send a copy of your logo to CPO so that they can use it on any publicity material they are producing for you.

☐ Many people are familiar with Scripture Union, especially in schools. If the event involves a Scripture Union evangelist or associate, including the Scripture Union logo on the publicity may encourage more people to support it.

CONTACT SCHOOLS

☐ Produce enough invitation cards to be distributed in each school (one card for every child in the school).

☐ Ask the head teacher (through the person liaising with the school) if he or she would be happy to distribute the cards for you.

☐ Deliver the cards to the school for distribution during the week prior to the event.

VISIT HOMES IN THE AREA

☐ Knock on doors and ask if there are children of the right age there. If so, leave invitation cards for them and a letter of explanation for the parents. (If school visits are not possible, knocking on doors is almost essential.)

LOCAL NEWS

☐ Make use of all other means of advertising the event, especially those that are free!

☐ Local newspapers (especially free ones) are always on the lookout for news (you shouldn't need to buy an ad).

☐ Make sure your article goes in about a month before the event begins.

☐ Local radio will often announce activities if you give them adequate warning.

CHECK YOUR CHURCH

☐ Stand outside your church building and try to imagine what it looks like to a visitor!

PUBLICITY

☐ Is it obvious what the church is called?

☐ If you only include the church's name on the publicity, will people know where to find it? Do you need to print the road name as well?

☐ Is it clear which door people should use to come in, or doesn't it matter?

☐ Does the church look attractive and inviting? Is the garden or graveyard well tended?

☐ Walk in through the door. Would a stranger feel welcome?

☐ Does it smell unpleasant? (One church I went to smelt of gas and boiled cabbage!)

YOUTH ACTIVITIES

☐ Youth events will need different publicity – don't try to combine the publicity for these with that for younger children.

There are prototype invitation cards, posters and other types of publicity on the following pages, which you can adapt and use.

A useful book about publicity and making the most of your church's image, is **Keep in touch!** by Peter Crumpler (Scripture Union).

ALL SAINTS CHURCH ANYTOWN

WHIZZ BANG!

(AGES 5–14)
MONDAY 2nd AUGUST
TO
FRIDAY 6th AUGUST
(Registration from 9.45am)

MORNING SESSION 10am–12pm
AFTERNOON SESSION 2–4pm

WEDNESDAY 4th AUGUST

MINI-WHIZZ
Under 5s only

MINI WHIZZ

CHURCH HALL
WEDNESDAY 2nd AUGUST
2.30pm until 4pm

PUPPETS SONGS CRAFTS

UNDER 5s AND MUMS AND DADS

FRIDAY WHIZZ

CHURCH HALL
FRIDAY AUGUST 7th
7.30pm–9pm

- Pizza
- Games
- Video

12 – 18s

FOR YOUNG PEOPLE

♪ Bring your friends! ♪

Rainbow Holiday Club

presents

SUPERCLUB

For Superkids
aged 3–10

Every day 10am to 12.30pm
Tuesday 30 Aug
to Friday 2 Sept

The Chapel
Sunny Road
West Side

More details phone
765 4321 (Wally)
234 4567 (Denise)

Supergames • Superstories • Superquizzes • Superprizes!!

Roll up, Roll up!

(Event name)

For children aged

(Ages)

(Times)

(Dates)

(Venue)

(Map)

(Contact details)

(A punchy, exciting message!)

PARENTING & RESOURCES

E V E N I N G

(Date/time)

An evening for parents, grandparents, in fact anyone with the care of children. A chance to talk, listen and look at a wide range of resources suitable for those bringing up children of all ages.

(Location map)

FAMILY EVENT

(Date/time)

An afternoon of fun in the Park for all the family followed by a Barbecue

Family Service

at

(Time)

(Venue)

(Date)

(Event name/logo)

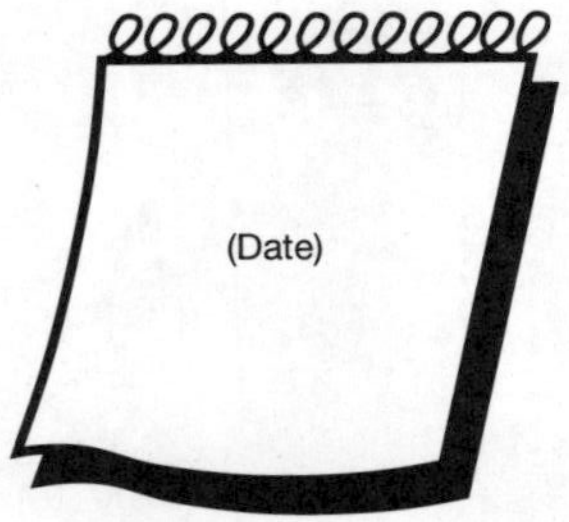

SPECIAL OFFER

FREE BADGE!

▼

when you come to

- -
(Event logo)

- -
(Date, time, venue)

Please bring this token with you

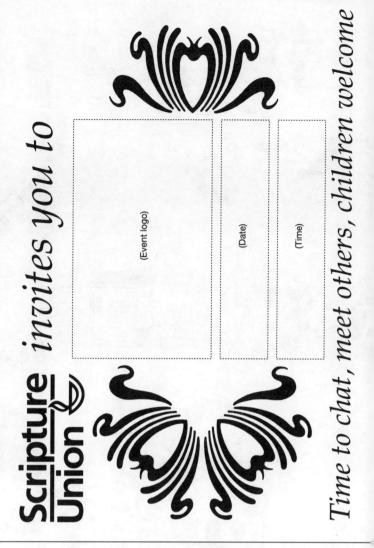

Scripture Union invites you to

(Event logo)

(Date)

(Time)

Time to chat, meet others, children welcome

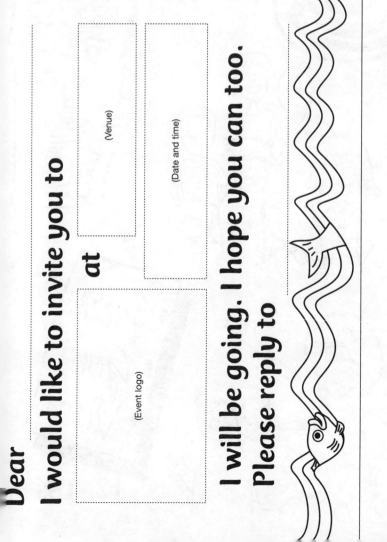

Dear

I would like to invite you to

at

(Venue)

(Date and time)

(Event logo)

I will be going. I hope you can too.

Please reply to

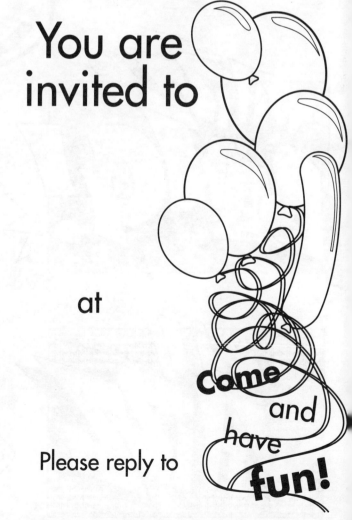

You are invited to

at

Please reply to

Come and have fun!

- - - - - - - - - - - - - -

SCHOOL LIAISON

ABOUT 3 MONTHS BEFORE, WRITE A LETTER

☐ Contact head teachers well in advance, especially if the event happens soon after the school holidays.

☐ There is a sample letter on D.2 to give you some idea of what to say. Head teachers are very busy, so be brief and to the point.

☐ If you are inviting a visiting evangelist to lead the event, he may have a leaflet describing what he offers to schools. Enclose the leaflet with your letter.

☐ Describe clearly what is being offered to the school.

☐ Ask if and when your visiting evangelist could come to the school (eg during the event).

PAY A VISIT

☐ After you have written, ask to meet the head teacher. Some heads agree to a visit immediately, others wish to consult with their staff or governors. If the latter is the case, offer to call back after a suitable interval for a decision.

☐ Be sure that you know what you are offering and what you are asking for, eg to take a school assembly, show a video or take RE lessons.

☐ Explain that you would like to make sure that all the children know they are invited to the event, so that none of them feel that they have missed out.

☐ Reassure the school that you will not pressurise children to come, and that you will make sure they check with their parents first.

☐ Mention that invitations are being printed for all the children in the area. Offer to give one to every child in the school. You will find that most head teachers will agree to give out the invitation cards for you. Some schools will distribute invitations even though they decline a visit.

☐ The school may have a system for sending items home, so check when you should take the cards in. Don't take them in too far in advance – certainly not more than a week before. Check how many will be required, if you don't already know.

☐ Offer posters if you can provide them.

MAKE A BOOKING

☐ Be sure to get all the details, especially if you are booking for someone else to visit. An outside evangelist would probably like to know:

  • the school's name, address and telephone number (and to have a map if possible)
  • the head's name (include his or her title – Mr/Mrs/Miss/Ms)
  • the number of staff and pupils in the school
  • the age range
  • the time and date of the booking

☐ Some head teachers may wish to discuss matters with the visiting evangelist in person. If possible, arrange for them to meet on the same day that you invite the evangelist to a planning meeting for the event. If the head teacher and evangelist are not able to meet, they can talk on the phone to make the final arrangements.

SCHOOL LIAISON

■ **SAMPLE LETTER TO HEAD TEACHER**

(Head teacher's name)
(School address)

(Special outreach event title)
(Dates)
(Age range)

Dear **(name)**

We have invited **(visiting evangelist's name)** to lead a special week for children at our church **(church name)** for the dates given above. **He/she** will be supported during the event by a team of helpers from our church.

The week is intended for all children in the age range, whether they presently attend church or not. We hope to make it a good week for all the community. Whilst the aim is to encourage children to continue coming to our own children's activities, we are firmly committed to ensuring that children already involved with other churches are encouraged to stay with those churches after the club.

(Visiting evangelist's name) is willing to visit schools, and I enclose a leaflet that outlines **his/her** involvement with churches and schools. I hope that **he/she** may be able to come to your school, as part of the week's activities.

We should be most grateful if, in due course, you would be willing to display a poster and distribute details about **(event name)** for us. Would it be possible for me to call in briefly to meet you? I should be glad to answer any questions you may have.

Yours sincerely

(Name)

THE PROGRAMME

SOME SAMPLE PROGRAMMES

A basic term-time club

6.00 pm The team arrives to pray and make any final preparations

6.20 pm Children arrive, register and go into their various groups for introductory activities

6.30 pm 'All together' time (the official start) for songs, prayers, quiz, memory verse, serial story and Bible story

7.10 pm Into groups to do funsheets based on the Bible story, craft activities, and so on

7.30 pm Children go home, the team prays together and clears up

An extended term-time club

5.30 pm Team arrives to pray and make final preparations

6.00 pm Children arrive, register and go into their groups for introductory activities

6.10 pm 'All together' time

6.50 pm Into groups for funsheets, etc

7.15 pm Puppets, drama or video

7.30 pm Children go home, the team prays together and clears up

A typical holiday club

9.00 am Team arrives, final preparation for setting up the hall, craft work, etc

9.30 am Bible study, prayer, last minute checks

10.00 am Children arrive, register, go to their groups and settle in

10.15 am Everyone comes together for a time of worship – songs, prayer, quiz, memory verse, serial story or Bible story

11.00 am Refreshments and a break

11.05 am Back into groups for funsheets (20 minutes) and crafts (40 minutes)

12.00 am Children go home, the team clears up, possibly lunch is provided, followed by a time of praise and evaluation

---

Games could be arranged for the afternoons, in the hall or in a nearby park, and one or two evenings could be set aside for the whole family, for a fun evening or to show a film. For games ideas, see **Over 300 Games for All Occasions** by Patrick Goodland (Scripture Union). For more ideas about the 'all together' times, see **Help! I Want to Tell Kids About Jesus** which has a chapter on each item, prayer, quiz, memory verse, Bible story, etc (obtainable from the Missions Department, Scripture Union; price at time of writing £3.00 including postage).

PEOPLE

NUMBERS

☐ Ideally, one adult for every eight children in a term-time club; holiday clubs with crafts need one adult for every five children. If possible, try to achieve the ratio of one adult for every four children.

OVERALL EVENT ORGANISERS

☐ Event co-ordinator

☐ Prayer organiser

☐ Publicity organiser

☐ Follow-up organiser

☐ Bible reading promoter

THE TEAM

☐ One group leader for every 6–8 children

☐ If anyone would rather just help with a group instead of lead, let them share a group with a leader

☐ One or preferably two 'up front' presenters (one of these might be a visiting evangelist) who should have no other major role during the event

☐ Alternatively, share the 'up front' presentation amongst the team, using the gifts that they have

☐ Musicians

☐ Actors/storytellers for the drama or Bible story

☐ Someone to organise the video and tape recorder and other technical equipment

☐ People to prepare refreshments for the team and for the children

☐ General team support

GETTING THE TEAM TOGETHER

☐ The event co-ordinator is the person likely to carry out the task of forming the team, though this may not always be the case. A group of people could take responsibility for doing this.

☐ Draw up a 'job description' beforehand, listing the qualities you are looking for. Circulate it among possible helpers, giving them plenty of time to pray and consider their response.

☐ Use the chart on F.4 to list group leaders and their helpers, noting the days they can and cannot help, to make sure that all the jobs are covered for every day of the event. It is best to do this by allocating people to an age group, and this chart will ensure that none of the age groups are forgotten.

☐ A visiting evangelist will need a copy of this list, as it will help him to get to know names and to know which group leader to send children to.

☐ The chart on F.5 lists the other jobs that need to be done and leaves space for you to write in people's names next to their allocated tasks. Don't panic if you can't fill all these jobs. Some of them can be done by those who are group leaders or group helpers if necessary.

PEOPLE

TEAM TASKS

Group leaders will be expected to:

☐ sit with their group during the 'all together' sessions and encourage the children to take part. This will make the task of leading these sessions much easier for the 'up front' presenter(s)

☐ be responsible for the children during the group times, build up relationships with them, help them to do any funsheets or activities, pray with them

☐ fill in club cards for the group, award prize points, etc

☐ develop friendships with parents and invite them to come to the family activities

☐ visit parents and invite them to church activities after the event is over (see TaskSheet G)

The Bible-reading promoter

☐ The Bible-reading promoter is responsible for encouraging children to think about Jesus by reading the Bible.

☐ The church might like to consider subsidising Bible reading notes or having introductory notes or 'Starters' available for children to take home, if they are interested. Scripture Union produces Bible reading notes for all ages. Contact the Scripture Union Marketing Department to find out what is available.

The welcoming committee

☐ Have a couple of people on door duty to greet the children with a smile, explain to them what to do and register them (see p 24).

☐ Until the start time, ask parents to take their children right into the building to join others of the same age in their groups. That way they hand the children over to their group leaders rather than just leaving them. This is safer and encourages parents to come in and see what's happening. Parents can stay with the children for a while to help them settle in. After the start they should just slip out at the back during the 'all together' activity.

☐ It may be good for someone to remain outside the door for a while after the event begins, to welcome latecomers and make sure children who have arrived don't get left outside.

☐ If parents arrive before the finish, have someone chat to them and assure them that the session will be over soon! Towards the end of the week they can invite parents to any family events you are planning.

Musicians

☐ Liaise with 'up front' presenters who may have particular songs they wish to use.

☐ Build up a band using the talent available, including those children who are willing to play.

☐ Collect together the music required. Contact Christian Copyright Licensing Limited, PO Box 1339, Eastbourne, East Sussex, BN21 4YF, telephone (01323) 417711, if permission to write up songs is needed.

PEOPLE

☐ Arrange, rearrange or transpose the music, as necessary.

☐ Practise together, possibly playing at the final team briefing, to teach songs to the team. Rehearsals should start at least 6 weeks before the event.

Actors/Storytellers

☐ Check through what is required with the event co-ordinator and the 'up front' presenters. Remember that some dramas need to be serious, some hilarious.

☐ Consider the suitability of scripts if they are being provided. Or write your own.

☐ Allocate the roles, drawing other people from the team if necessary.

'Up front' presenter(s)

☐ Study the programme carefully to familiarise yourself with the event theme and all the activities.

☐ Plan the 'all together' times. Consider including songs, prayer, Bible stories, quizzes, memory verses, drama or puppets, joke spots, making up chants or cheers, aerobics, putting a team member 'on the spot' (ie asking questions about their faith), competitions, and so on.

☐ Think about using other team members, to make use of their gifts and to share the spotlight.

☐ Collect the necessary equipment together.

☐ Check the amplification levels of your venue if necessary.

☐ Liaise with the musicians over songs.

Craft organiser

☐ Study the theme material, making a note of the craft ideas presented or inventing your own. Keep these simple, especially if other team members have to organise them.

☐ Collect together the required materials – glue, egg-boxes, etc. The church will love saving their loo-roll centres for you, even if you don't need them!

☐ Collect together the necessary equipment – scissors, paints, pencils, etc. Liaise with the visiting evangelist, if there is one, to save buying equipment that he or she can provide.

☐ Explain the crafts to the team at the final briefing, or at a separate session where everyone can make their own samples. Be sure to have one that you made earlier!

Here's one I made earlier by Kathryn Copsey (Scripture Union) has many great ideas for crafts for 3–11s.

PEOPLE AND THEIR JOBS

Event co-ordinator

Prayer secretary

Schools liaison

Follow-up organiser

Bible reading promoter

'All together' session leaders

Group leaders and helpers

Cross out any ages or days that don't apply, or combine them by drawing a circle around them if you wish. Try to get a minimum of two people per age group each day. One person could be the group leader, the other a group helper. If you are expecting a lot of children, try to get four people for each age group. Obviously, it is better if the same group leaders can be with the same children every day, though sometimes this will not be possible.

Age groups	Mon	Tues	Wed	Thurs	Fri	Sat	Sun
4 years							
5 years							
6 years							
7 years							
8 years							
9 years							
10 years							
11 years							
12 years							

PEOPLE AND THEIR JOBS

Welcoming
committee
(minimum
two people)

_____

_____

Setting up the
technical equipment
(video, sound
system, etc)

_____

_____

Bookstall organiser

_____

_____

Badge machine
operator

_____

Refreshment
team

_____

_____

_____

_____

People to help with
setting up and packing
away (either daily or
at the start and end
of the event)

_____

_____

_____

Road Safety
Patrol

_____

_____

Musicians

_____

_____

_____

_____

_____

_____

_____

General team
support

_____

Actors/storytellers

_____

_____

_____

_____

_____

_____

_____

_____

_____

_____

_____

_____

FOLLOW-UP

THE MAIN TASKS

☐ To follow-up the children or parents who respond to the spiritual message of the event

☐ To invite children who don't yet go to any church activities to come and join in

☐ To involve and co-ordinate the whole church in the task of follow-up

I'D LIKE TO INVITE YOU TO...'

☐ Have special invitation cards printed listing regular church activities that are appropriate for the children and families who have come to the special outreach event.

☐ Visit every child who comes to the event and give them an invitation the week after it is over and still fresh in people's minds.

☐ Parents should be invited personally by people from the church rather than through a card or letter sent home with their children. Make sure that each non-church family receives a visit. Perhaps each group leader could visit with a personal invitation.

A QUESTIONNAIRE

☐ Use the sample questionnaire on G.3 to help people 'break the ice' when visiting. It should also give an idea of the numbers interested in coming to further activities on a regular basis.

☐ At the bottom of the questionnaire (or on a separate leaflet) you might add a list of church activities so that team members have the correct times to give to those they visit.

☐ When the questionnaires have been gathered in, take time to examine the responses so as to plan for the future.

☐ Consider running other activities for children than those you run at present. Sometimes Sunday is a visiting day for non-church people, so sending their children to church on a Sunday morning may not be convenient. The questionnaire gives people a chance to suggest a better time. Many churches are now running a week-night club once a week.

A useful book for ideas on what to do to start a week-night club is **Help! I Want to Tell Kids About Jesus** (from Missions Department, Scripture Union, price £3.00 including postage).

CHRISTIAN BASICS COURSE

☐ On the questionnaire you could include a question asking parents if they would like to know more about the Christian faith. Why not take a booklet for them to read with you, or invite them to join a Christian basics course?

☐ If you have been building up contacts in your area for a while, this may be the right time to offer such a course, which could take place in someone's home.

☐ Think carefully about the kind of course you are offering. It must suit the people you are inviting. It should be a non-threatening opportunity to discuss and talk through Christian issues.

FOLLOW-UP

THE NEXT STEP

☐ If you are running your own outreach event, think through at the planning stage how you will encourage children to respond to the gospel in ways that are appropriate.

☐ Offer a response card to all children who are interested. Make a note of their names so that the children can be followed up.

☐ After the event is over, a number of children will have indicated various responses. Children may have:

- taken the response cards but have gone no further
- told you that they have prayed the prayer on the response card
- asked lots of questions
- told you that they are already friends of Jesus

Consider inviting them all to meet together to talk about being friends of Jesus. You might use Bible reading notes for their age group as a basis for your meeting, or you could work out a short series of 'Christian basics for children' to use with them.

☐ If you have a visiting evangelist, he or she may be able to recommend a booklet to help children make their response.

There is a prototype response card on the facing page. The tear-off section of the card has space for group leaders to write details about where children can send for further information about following Jesus.

'OPERATION BARNABAS'

☐ One 'way in' to encouraging children (and their parents) to become friends of Jesus is to link each new Christian with someone who can help them – a 'Barnabas'. He or she can explain about following Jesus, introduce the new Christian to the church (as Barnabas did Paul, Acts 9:27), and provide encouragement (Acts 4:36). This is especially important for children from non-Christian families, who need more support than usual to help them go on following Jesus.

Further information and ideas are provided in a book called **Operation Barnabas** which is available from the Scripture Union Missions Department (send £1.00 + 30p postage for your copy). This is a small book written for adults who want to help children become friends of Jesus. You may like to read through **Operation Barnabas** first, and then decide how many of the leaders ought to have a copy to prepare themselves for helping children in the ways suggested. **Operation Barnabas** also gives ideas for what to do after the event to help children carry on being friends of Jesus.

Jesus wants us to be his friends because he really loves us.
If you become Jesus' friend, he has promised to forgive you for everything you have done wrong and to be with you always.

HOW CAN I ASK JESUS TO BE MY FRIEND?

☐ You need to thank God for loving you and sending his Son, Jesus.

☐ You need to say sorry for the wrong things you have done, and be sure you don't want to do them again.

☐ You must believe that Jesus died on the cross so that people could be forgiven for the wrong things they have done.

If you are sorry and do believe this, here is a prayer you can say:

Dear Lord Jesus, I'm sorry for all the things I have done wrong. Thank you for loving me. Thank you for coming into the world and dying on a cross for me. Please forgive me and be my friend. Please send your Holy Spirit to help me be friends with you for the rest of my life and to do the things that please you. Amen.

Jesus hears us when we pray to him and has promised to forgive us and help us be friends with him, if we want to. If you have really meant this prayer… you are now one of Jesus' friends!
Once you are his friend, you will want to please him. But all of us let him down sometimes. When you do, DON'T WORRY! Remember:

✓ **Jesus has forgiven you.**

✓ **His Holy Spirit is there to help you.**

✓ **He will always be your friend – and he wants you to be his friend – forever!**

You may like to write your name here, in case you lose this card and want it to be returned to you.

Name
_____

Age
_____

If you want to be a friend of Jesus, we would like to know about it so that we can help you! Please fill in the section below, cut it off and give it back to the person who gave you this card.

Name _____ **Age** _____

Address _____

Postcode _____

Or write to

FOLLOW-UP QUESTIONNAIRE

QUESTIONNAIRE

(Church name)

This questionnaire is to assist us in evaluating ....
and in deciding the best form of regular activities for the children and families
who have taken part. Thank you for letting your child(ren) attend.

How did you hear about .... ? ☐ School   ☐ Church friends   ☐ Other
                  (Name of event)

Did your child(ren) enjoy .... ? ☐ Yes   ☐ No
              (Name of event)

If yes, do you know what they enjoyed most? ....

If no, what didn't they enjoy, or wish that we had included? ....

If your child doesn't come to our regular Sunday/mid-week
church activities for children, would they like to come?   ☐ Yes   ☐ No

At the moment our church runs ....
                      (Name of activity)

at .... on ....
  (Time)   (Day)

Is this a convenient day and time for your child(ren) to attend?   ☐ Yes   ☐ No

If not, what would be a more convenient time? ....

Is there any other activity that you or members of your family would like our church to organise or assist with?

Are there any comments you would like to add? ....

Thank you for taking time to respond to this questionnaire.

(List of church activities)

CATERING

DURING A HOLIDAY CLUB

☐ Allow time in the middle of your holiday club programme to serve drinks and biscuits to the children and tea or coffee to the team.

☐ If children bring a packed lunch, have them put their lunch boxes in a safe area, perhaps a place near their groups.

☐ Make one day of the club special by inviting children to stay to lunch. In rural areas they might have to stay to lunch every day, especially if you are planning an afternoon programme as well.

☐ If you provide lunch for the children, things like hot-dogs are very popular and quite simple to prepare. Sandwiches seem to go down less well. Ice cream cones are good for dessert. Avoid anything that involves too much washing up!

☐ Make sure that food hygiene requirements are followed when storing and preparing food. Plastic cups, plates or cutlery will increase the cost but save on washing-up time.

☐ Why not lay on lunch for team members and their families at the end of busy holiday club mornings? This saves people having to go home at lunch-time. In one church I visited, a lady who didn't want to work with the children offered to make soup and rolls for all the team. It was a lovely home-made soup, and it certainly added to our fellowship together as a team!

DURING A TERM-TIME CLUB

☐ Refreshments in the middle of a programme are not normally necessary for term-time events unless the children come straight from school. However, a hot drink and a biscuit for each team member at the end of a term-time club are a great idea.

☐ Why not provide refreshments for parents who arrive early to pick up their children, to make them feel more welcome?

☐ If team members are coming straight from work to help with the event, it would be good to offer them something to keep them going, perhaps a light meal. Organise this so that team members who would like food sign up for it – refreshments for everyone at the start tends to cause delay and distract people from getting on with praying and being ready for the event.

FAMILY FOOD

☐ During a family fun event, refreshments are a good way of allowing people to sit and chat as they eat. What you provide will depend on the time available and your resources. If your family event is in the early evening, a cup of tea or coffee and a biscuit will often suffice. But you may like to offer more, perhaps a barbecue or a 'finger buffet'. This could include sausage rolls, mini samosas, cheese and pineapple chunks on sticks, crisps, peanuts, little cakes and biscuits. Predicting the numbers of people who will come to these events can be difficult. Choose refreshments that can be stretched to fit however many people there are.

Some churches are brilliant at looking after visiting speakers. Others just don't seem to have thought it through. A visiting evangelist's requirements are generally modest, but they do like to be asked about them!

Hospitality

Evangelists with young families may not wish to stay for a whole week. If they did this for every special outreach event, they would be in danger of hardly ever being at home. It is much safer to assume that they will not stay. However, if the event is a long way from an evangelist's home and there are late nights and early starts, he or she would probably appreciate the offer of being put up overnight. Or if there are school visits early in the morning and the club is in the evening, it would be nice to invite them for lunch. If the club is in the early evening, note that some visitors might prefer not to have too much to eat just before it.

Preparation

Most speakers do the bulk of their preparation before the event. There just isn't time once it all starts. Each day some time will be needed to make sure everything is set up. For example, I like to be able to get into the church at least an hour before the programme begins each day.

One host at a church I visited had a great idea. He was a minister, so perhaps he understood better than some. He offered me a bedroom in his house to be quiet in. If I went there, I would be left alone to prepare, meditate or sleep. I was also welcome to sit in the lounge where people would come and talk with me. Visiting speakers often need both options!

Local knowledge

Please don't assume your visitor will pick everything up at once. He or she probably won't remember who everyone is, even though you have introduced them once. A visitor may be working with many churches in a year. I ask people, leaders as well as children, to wear badges to help with this.

Provide your visitor with a street map of your area if you can. It is a good reassurance if they get lost or have to find a number of homes or schools. If your church or area has a special local name, do tell them. If certain people need to be treated with care (either in the church or outside), don't let the visitor blunder in.

Keys

It is a great help to offer a key to a visiting evangelist who has a lot of equipment in your church. This frees them from having to find someone each time they need something or want to set up.

Keep your visitor informed

I have arrived for planning meetings, all ready to talk about one programme of activities, to be told that the church had changed their mind and now wanted another! It is helpful to keep an up-to-date record of decisions agreed and provide your visitor with a copy. I now make notes at meetings and always confirm details with the church to make sure.

Sharing and learning

As I mentioned earlier, one of the dangers of inviting a visiting evangelist is that the children become attached to him or her and don't come again when the event is over! This is why it is a good idea for the church to provide most of the team. It is also good to share the leading of some of the 'all together' time between the evangelist and local church members. People may be shy about doing the 'up front' activities when a visitor is there. I sometimes get told, 'You do it, you're better than us' or 'You're a hard act to follow!' My answer is that everyone has to learn sometime. If an evangelist wasn't at least reasonable at this sort of thing, you would be disappointed and sorry that you ever invited one! I try to mix showing how I think it should be done with encouraging others to have a go. Perhaps the person coming after a visitor could be ready to continue with the same songs, quizzes and other ideas as the visitor. This will help to give the children some sort of sense of continuity.

In the final analysis, anything done together as a team, concentrated over a few days, will always seem more exciting than regular weekly activities. You can't keep up the concentrated effort. Your visiting evangelist couldn't. So don't be too disappointed. Prepare and plan to do your best.

Afterwards

A visiting speaker always likes to know what has happened as a result of his visit, so please don't forget to let them know.

■ Badges

Try your local play resource centre; they may have a badge machine you can borrow. If you want to buy a badge machine yourself, I recommend Enterprise Products, 36 Ridgeway Road, Redhill, Surrey, RH1 6PH, telephone (01737) 772185. They are fairly inexpensive and the machines are light and easy to use. They also make key rings and mirrors.

■ Barn dancing

For books and tapes, contact The English Folk Dance and Song Society, Cecil Sharp House, 2 Regents Park Road, London, NW1 7AY, telephone 0171 284 0534.

■ Bibles, Gospels

At a reduced price (only for giving away): Bible Society, Stonelea Green, Westlea, Swindon, SN5 7DG.

■ Bunting, flags, party hats, wigs, party stuff

Barnums, 67 Hammersmith Road, London, W14 8UY.

■ Christian Copyright Licensing Limited,

PO Box 1339, Eastbourne, East Sussex, BN21 4YF, telephone (01323) 417711.

■ Films, videos

International Films, 235 Shaftesbury Avenue, London, WC2H 8EL. Videos and tapes can also be obtained from Scripture Union Mail Order (see below).

■ Games

The Great Play Times Games Kit can be obtained from The National Playing Fields Association, 25 Ovington Square, London, SW3 1LQ. This is a card index full of games, organised into various sections.

■ Parachutes

These can be bought from the Missions Department, Scripture Union (see below), or Bee Tee Products Ltd, Cemetery Lane, Carlton, Wakefield, West Yorkshire, WF3 3QT, telephone (01532) 824494, fax no. (01532) 824706. They can also be borrowed from Scripture Union evangelists or from play resource centres.

■ Pens and pencils

Inscribed with text, club name: Park Advertising, The Bungalow, Hough, Stump Cross, Halifax, West Yorkshire, HX3 7AP.

■ Plastic bags, re-sealable bags, plastic sheets

Transatlantic Plastics, 23–25 Brighton Road, Surbiton, Surrey, KT6 5LR.

■ Printing

For reasonable cost and good quality from a Christian printer, try The Doron Press, 14 Greenhalgh Moss Lane, Bury, Lancashire, BL8 1TZ, telephone (0161) 761 3916.

■ Publicity

CPO, Garcia Estate, Canterbury Road, Worthing, Sussex, BN13 1BW, telephone (01903) 264556.

■ Scripture Union

207–209 Queensway, Bletchley, Milton Keynes, Buckinghamshire, MK2 2EB, telephone (01908) 856000; fax no. (01908) 856111.

■ Scripture Union Training Unit

26–30 Heathcoat Street, Nottingham, NG1 3AA, telephone (0115) 9418144; fax no. (0115) 9414624.

■ Scripture Union Mail Order

P.O. Box 764, Oxford, OX4 5FJ, telephone (01865) 747669.

■ Tarpaulins

For children to sit on, especially outdoors or in a marquee. One supplier is Bradshaws Tarpaulins, Clifton Industrial Estate, York, YO3 8XX, telephone (01904) 691169.

You will find suppliers in your area in the **Yellow Pages** or the classified ads section in local newspapers. Where appropriate, ask for competitive quotations to be sure you are getting value for money.

SCRIPTURE UNION BOOK LIST

Become Like a Child, Kathryn Copsey
The Bumper Book of Family Activities, John Marshall
Family Evangelism, John Hattam (obtainable from the
    Missions Department)
Help! I Want to Tell Kids About Jesus, Steve Hutchinson
    (obtainable from the Missions Department)
Help! There's a Child in my Church, Peter Graystone
Here's One I Made Earlier, Kathryn Copsey
Keep in Touch, Peter Crumpler
Reaching Children and Reaching Families, Paul Butler
Operation Barnabas (obtainable from the Missions
    Department)
Outside In, Mike Breen
Over 300 Games for All Occasions, Patrick Goodland
Under-Fives Welcome!, Kathleen Crawford